WRITING THE QUALITATIVE DISSERTATION:
Understanding by Doing

WRITING THE
QUALITATIVE DISSERTATION:
Understanding by Doing

Judith M. Meloy
Castleton State College

LEA LAWRENCE ERLBAUM ASSOCIATES, PUBLISHERS

1994 Hillsdale, New Jersey Hove, UK

Lawrence Erlbaum Associates, Publishers
365 Broadway
Hillsdale, New Jersey 07642

Cover design by Mairav Salomon-Dekel

Library of Congress Cataloging-in-Publication Data

Meloy, Judith M.
Writing the qualitative dissertation : understanding by doing /
Judith M. Meloy
p. cm.
Includes bibliographical references and index.
ISBN 0-8058-1416-7 (cloth). — ISBN 0-8058-1417-5 (pbk.)
1. Dissertations, Academic—Handbooks, manuals, etc. 2.
Research—Handbooks, manuals, etc. I. Title.
LB2369.M38 1994
808'.02 dc20   93-35958
                                                            CIP

Books published by Lawrence Erlbaum Associates are printed on
acid-free paper, and their bindings are chosen for strength and dura-
bility.

Printed in the United States of America
10 9 8 7 6 5 4 3

CONTENTS

RESEARCH CORRESPONDENTS

Lew Allen, EdD (1992)

Anonymous

"Ann," a doctoral student

"Carol," EdD (1989)

Robert M. Foster, EdD (1988)

Pat M. Garlikov, PhD (1990)

Patricia Kovel-Jarboe, PhD (1986)

Timothy McCollum, graduate student

Marie Wilson Nelson, EdD (1982)

Kristin Park, PhD (1992)

Jane F. Patton, EdD (1991)

Paula Gastenveld Payne, EdD (1990)

Maria Piantanida, PhD (1982)

Gretchen S. Rauschenberg, PhD (1986)

Kathy Rojek, EdD (1991)

Helen Rolfe, PhD (1990)

Kathryn A. Scherck, DNSc, RN (1989)

Stuart J. Sigman, PhD (1982)

Jean M. Stevenson, PhD (1989)

Nancy Zeller, PhD (1987)

FOREWORD

I was really pleased to see that you hope to include some more detailed letters in your book. What I find exciting about your research is that you'll include as much of our voice as possible the voice and concerns of people doing or recently finished doing qualitative research. I think I said Bogdan and Biklen (1982) was my favorite all-round decision rules and example book, but it's still several steps removed from actual experience—what we wanted to know and what we wanted changed, what we did.

Ann, correspondent
February 11, 1991

The draft of your text has been extremely helpful to me at this juncture of my work. I have just begun to dig into the Ely (1991) book; both are an important part of jogging my spirit into the "running" mode necessary to produce the big "D"....I come away from this reading with so many emotions—I can definitely see the value in correspondence and dialogue with others who have been through the maze.

Carolyn Gabb, graduate student
July 26, 1992

Judith, I can send more information to you should you need more. I would also be pleased to work with you in any form or fashion for this project. I think it is an important one. I believe in qualitative research. It has more 'meaning' to me than statistical data, although I know statistics are important. More books (like Lincoln & Guba's 1985 book) are needed to guide faculty and students in qualitative research decisions. Certainly, it would have helped me!.... Happy writing!

Paula Payne, EdD, correspondent
December 3, 1990

I would love to have had your book while doing my dissertation.

Kathryn Scherck, DNSc, RN, correspondent
September 3, 1990

ACKNOWLEDGMENTS

First, I would like to thank the publisher and the anonymous reviewers of this book for their time and encouragement. I also want to thank Stuart Sigman, who is a correspondent in this study. He not only read and critiqued an early draft of this material, but also helped me find our publisher.

Thanks also go to Carolyn Gabb and Egon Guba. Carolyn provided a useful and detailed commentary on an earlier draft of this book from her perspective as a doctoral student doing qualitative research for her dissertation. Egon Guba challenged me to think, risk, understand, and do during my graduate assistantship and doctoral studies; he also supported those efforts. Only since the completion of my doctoral work do I fully appreciate the opportunity I had. Thanks, Egon.

I want to thank my mom and dad, Mimi and John Meloy. They are especially fine people, who taught me a lot about being human. For their generosity of spirit and unconditional love, I am forever blessed.

Finally, I want to thank each of the correspondents. I would especially like to thank my good friend Pat Garlikov, whom I met when she was an eager doctoral student seeking information on how to do qualitative research. Pat has talked with me throughout the evolution of this manuscript; her keen insights have not been ignored. I am also fortunate to know Kathy, Helen, and Nancy; I have spoken with most of the others on the phone. For further information about them, see Appendix B.

Judith M. Meloy

Introduction

One of the most common ways we have of learning to do something is by doing it. But unlike fastening our shoes or baking a cake—processes that have been simplified by the introduction of velcro and "just add oil" mixes—'doing' research is becoming more complex and controversial. Although qualitative researchers are making substantial contributions to scholarship by describing not only how research is conceptualized but also how its 'products' are finally presented and understood, there is, for novice researchers and traditionally trained faculty members across the wide array of disciplines, a down side. As the number of methodological options and alternative presentations of research increase, so does the ambiguity for those who will be answering questions such as:

- Which paradigm, methodology, or methods do I use?
- What are the particular standards (philosophical, practical) for doing qualitative research?
- What exactly is meant by 'qualitative research'?
- What is the basis for the analysis and interpretation of experience?
- How does any chosen option enable 'justifiable', rigorous research?
- What will the presentation of the research look like?

As I listen to my peers or curious doctoral students, it is still the case that not all interested inquirers are getting direct, in-depth support for learning about qualitative research. For example, I received the following request for the paper I presented at the 1992 conference of the American Educational Research Association (AERA):

June 8, 1992

Dear Dr. Meloy:

I am beginning to write a qualitative dissertation for a Ph.D....I'll conduct ethnographic interviews and I want to sustain as much rigor as possible in the qualitative aspects of the design. Will you help me?...I've gleaned a great deal of information about qualitative research from presenters at former AERA conventions by using microfiches....

I am genuinely concerned about the limited scope of this student's learning experience. I do not know if this person will have additional opportunities to study qualitative research methodology; the current mode of learning is clear.

In response to the request, I mailed out a short bibliography, a synthesis from my own experiences and those of my correspondents, whose reflections comprise the basis of this book. Included on that list are books such as Marshall and Rossman's (1989) *Designing Qualitative Research* and Lincoln and Guba's (1985) *Naturalistic Inquiry*. These authors and others present, from the conception of the problem to the final interpretations, how to go about doing qualitative research. In contrast, the purpose of this book is to share, in rich detail, understandings of how it <u>feels</u> and what it <u>means</u> to do qualitative research for the doctoral dissertation.

Why This Book?

Two experiences compelled me to compile and offer this book. The first was my own doctoral dissertation research experience, which fostered the idea. I emerged from those months during the spring of 1986 with a set of recurring questions, concerns, feelings, and needs that have not gone away. As I was working, I was sure that others choosing to use qualitative methodologies were going through similar periods of doubt and euphoria. I was also sure that guidelines existed somewhere, that is, that someone had already interpreted for the novice what it meant to work through an emergent design from proposal to final defense, someone had thought about what it meant—as a student and human being—to be the research 'instrument' of choice. I was sure that <u>somebody</u> could describe how the form of a qualitative dissertation—from the statement of the problem through the presentation of the data and the analysis and interpretation of results—differed from a traditional five chapter, third person thesis. But I was unable to find "the" exemplar to help me. What I did find were several examples of 'qualitative' theses that had been written and successfully defended at Indiana University before mine. What seemed clear, however, after working through the experience for myself, was that the overall format and internal structure of qualitative dissertations were different from those that had come before.

The second experience and catalyst for writing this book has been my participation at the Qualitative Research in Education conference sponsored by the School of Education at the University of Georgia. I have listened to the stories of graduate students and faculty members who, alone and cooperatively, have been working through what it means to do qualitative research. I have heard questions, confusions, answers, interpretations, joys, and sorrows. I have seen how eagerly graduate students have wanted to share and get support for what they were trying to figure out and accomplish. I have heard faculty members seeking fuller understanding so that they could interact positively with their students, because it is not, as one correspondent writes, "as easy as it looks."

During the past 6 years, although I have continued to learn a lot, I remain intuitively (if not logically and philosophically) convinced that we need to better understand the interrelationships of the processes of qualitative research. The conscious and tacit learning-thinking-researching-feeling-knowing and writing—the simultaneous and multifaceted processes of inquiry—ensure the integrity of the qualitative research effort. Indeed, that is why I separated the actions in the previous sentence with hyphens instead of commas; the workings are connected and multiple rather than discrete and linear. They imply more than one level of processing at a time. The complexity of the researcher as the human instrument has only begun to be explicated.

Doing qualitative research for one's thesis requires a conscious, internal awareness within the external structural, political, and human context of higher education, because the dissertation is the focus of intense personal interaction and ambiguity around such tasks as forming a dissertation committee or choosing an area of interest. The correspondents, whose reflections are the data source for this book, describe some of the interactions and sources of ambiguity that are a part of the process of qualitative research and hence of concern to doctoral students choosing qualitative research methodologies for their thesis research.

About the Study

In order to find others who could provide additional perspectives on the experience, I placed a notice in *The Chronicle of Higher Education* in March 1990, asking individuals who had used qualitative methodologies in their dissertations to write me. While I was waiting for a response to the request, I undertook an Educational Resources Information Center (ERIC) search to locate individuals who used the words "qualitative" or "naturalistic" as theses' descriptors. I located almost 80 authors through the dissertation abstracts.

Between April and June I received 70 inquiries from the *Chronicle* notice; I was also able to match 35 names from the dissertation abstracts to the current roster of faculty members in higher education. To each of these 105 persons I mailed a letter, explaining my curiosity about the format and structure of their dissertations (see Appendix A). I asked specific questions: Did you use first or third person in your thesis? How many chapters did you have? Why? What sources were invaluable to you? What assumptions did you make? Did you keep a journal? I asked them to write me a letter, pertaining to these or any other decision rules they made that resulted in the final form of their theses.

By September 1990, I had received 12 letters. I sent an update letter to everyone, proposing my schedule of analysis, writing, and publishing; I gave them some additional time to respond. By December 1, 1990, I had 18 responses, 16 of which were letters of some length with supporting documents. During the annual Qualitative Research in Education conference sponsored by the School of Education at the University of Georgia in January 1991, I was able to collect additional information from another 30 or so people who attended an interactive workshop on the topic. By mid-January 1991, I was ready to begin with the contributions of 20 individuals; 6 were graduate students and 14 were PhDs and EdDs at the time of the writing. Their dissertations are in the fields of communication, education, geology, nursing, and sociology. By May 1991, the first draft of this book was completed and the search for a publisher had begun.

Audience

The target audience for this book is and always has been doctoral students. Those of us who have gone through the experience have something to offer those who will choose to do so. I believe that a book offering a variety of perspectives on what it means and feels like to do qualitative research for the doctoral dissertation provides an alternative conception of support not unlike Ely's (1991) *Doing Qualitative Research: Circles within Circles* and Glesne and Peshkin's (1992) *Becoming Qualitative Researchers: An Introduction.* In addition, I believe that faculty members and friends of qualitative researchers can better appreciate some of the dilemmas facing novice qualitative researchers as a result of reading this book. I have written it with this secondary audience in mind as well.

Perspectives

Each individual reader will bring his or her own experiences and expectations to this book. At one level, the material may be regarded as a compilation of "war stories," the thick description and recollection of a particular experience from a variety of perspectives. The question of "so what?" is answered by acknowledging that we do learn vicariously from other people's experience; we also feel about their experiences and learn from those feelings. Our cognition and feelings combine in ways that enable us as individuals to regard our contemporary experiencing from a variety of perspectives, and hence judge it, hone it, foster it, or reshape it. Depending on who the reader is and his or her individual context, certain episodes will 'mean' more than others, and certain caveats or suggestions will seem more salient. Nevertheless, the correspondents' reflections may focus, enable, or guide both doctoral students and dissertation committee members in their conversations around qualitative research issues (Morgan, 1983). Finally, although I do not interpret my role as qualitative researcher and writer to be that of a judge ruling on the experiences of my correspondents, I do have professional concerns about some of the experiences they described. I indicate these concerns as they appear throughout the book and summarize them in the final chapter. I hope that some of the issues raised will encourage the continuation of the concerned dialogue about the qualities and quality of qualitative research.

Style and Structure

Style

My predisposition in this volume is to be informal. I have had many one-on-one conversations with doctoral students and faculty members; you has always been the form of address (i.e., "What are you thinking?" or "How are you managing?") I will try not to be too comfortable with you, the reader, but I do not want a formal tone to block the personal and personable nature of this research. The data are letters; my correspondents and I came to know each other through the mail. Together we are thinking and sharing out loud. I want the correspondents to speak to you in the same way; it is for this reason that I most often use the present tense when citing them.

In most cases, I use the correspondents' first names with their contributions; whenever I thought the material might be harmful, I deleted any attribution. We went back and forth about this; I have at least three pledges from each of them (see Appendix A). My correspondents stand by their reflections; my final decision, however, has been to provide anonymity around certain issues in order to enable the issue to take precedence over where and with whom it occurred. In addition, each correspondent had several opportunities to edit the materials I have included in this book. I was more cautious than they were; I remain responsible for any errors in judgment.

In order to provide a sense of the research context as I experienced it, I include some lengthy excerpts from the correspondents' letters that contain more than one point. I have not tried to select out the point that I think the correspondents are making. I have also tried not to reduce their contributions to the particular sense that I want to make. I also try to keep possible meanings open by placing single quotation marks around certain words that either 'feel' ambiguous to me or may have different meanings for the reader. Sometimes I use hyphens to separate thoughts. Many of the correspondents' letters also share these stylistic informalities.

I do clarify the points that I used to connect the experiences of the correspondents together; I hope this will not stop you from finding different points of interest or debate, or a different sense of the 'whole'. I believe this book will enable all of us to become more consciously aware of the complex issues and nuances of 'qualitative' decision making. If I have accomplished presenting a range of experiences, then I believe that this book will become your volume of conclusions and sense rather than one by the correspondents and me. The book is meant as a means rather than an end, as an offering rather than an imperative.

Structure

The organization of the chapters emerged from my interest in providing support for the processes of qualitative research. The processes are foundational to the whole of the research experience, although understanding that whole rarely happens until the end of a work. Therefore, I chose to begin this book with a chapter about "the end," where an amount of certainty and confidence finally emerges for the novice qualitative researcher. In addition, I pose a set of QUESTIONS in each chapter that became explicit as a result of my interaction with the correspondents' ideas. These questions extend beyond the original focusing ones of this study and can be considered a part of my analysis process. The questions are, in a strict sense, neither solved nor answered. I will disappoint all readers who are looking for the "right" answers. I also do not presume that the questions are unique or original. However, I do intend, by asking them here, to locate the questions in one place in explicit, written form. I believe that these questions will prod you to consider the totality of the research endeavor as you encounter seemingly discrete concerns.

I also chose, finally, to use headings to provide additional focus points. I believe that the headings themselves are <u>arbitrary</u>; the themes of the correspondents' letters run into each other throughout this book. Other points in the letters offer additional concerns. However, because headings can serve to reduce initial ambiguity, I believe that they may be of some use here.

In a critique of an earlier draft of some of this material, an anonymous reviewer stated, "I really don't see much of a point to all of this except, perhaps, to make the qualitative researcher 'feel good.'" It seems to me that this objective is a fundamentally humane and worthy purpose for this book. I welcome your comments and concerns.

1

UNDERSTANDING BY FINISHING:
The End is the Beginning

Although I was never alone in my graduate research classes, I found that I was always alone as I was collecting and analyzing data for my thesis. I did not have the companionship of an a priori hypothesis or a statistical design to guide and structure me. None of my courses had required the intense interaction between doing and thinking on such sustained and multiple levels. With the general focus of my dissertation taped on the wall in front of my desk, I continuously had to attend to the tangents of analysis, letting them play themselves out in order to understand which paths, if any, were worth pursuing, or if the emerging foci or, indeed, the general one with which I began needed adjusting. I was alone with notes all over the place—organized chaos—and yet never alone, as there were always thoughts sprouting in a brain partially numbed to anything but them. I had no idea what 'doing all of this' meant and, at times, if I could do it at all. It was like struggling with a team of wild horses pulling a runaway wagon.

Because the efforts to understand and manage my thesis research are as memorable as the substance of the thesis itself, I am convinced that neither course work and texts about how to understand and do qualitative research nor the beginnings of my own efforts to learn by doing would be the appropriate starting point for a book about the <u>experiencing</u> of such things. Those of us who have completed at least one major research project using qualitative methodologies have learned that it is only AT THE END of the experience that we begin to see the whole we constructed. To committees and graduate students, such last minute knowledge is not yet acceptable—"What are the a priori foci?" and "What will you have when you are finished?" are examples of questions that we have been led to believe we should be able to answer from the very beginning.

BY THE END of the dissertation experience I was able to explain why the thesis looked like it did. At the beginning, I did not understand the concept of "being able to handle ambiguity" in any practical way. I had a sense of the practicalities of working with a committee of four different individuals but did not actually know what to expect. At the beginning, I did not know how different from my ordinary ways of making sense of the world the dissertation research process was going to be. In spite of my course work, I had no idea of what it felt like to do research. Writing the dissertation was an experience in itself; adding qualitative research on top of that made for an especially interesting time of learning, reflection, and practice. I often felt like I was playing a game of pickup sticks while balancing on a high wire over an empty river in the middle of a moonless night.

What does a qualitative dissertation look like at THE END? Will reading about a variety of structures for qualitative dissertations and the processes novice qualitative researchers used to formulate these structures help as you begin your efforts? Is there some target formula or structure that doctoral students should aim for and committee members expect? From the material I have collected, the only certainty exists in a range of possibilities often determined by a combination of factors including subject matter, personal background (including education and individual judgment), committee input, methodological implications, and so on.

Format Options

Process Influences

Most correspondents answered my question about the number of chapters in their dissertation. The nuance I found interesting in the following two selections is the manner in which both Pat and Carol expressed their answers. Pat writes, "I ended up with 7 chapters. I followed a non-traditional, 7 chapter approach including a final summary. My appendices include the transcribed episodes, content analysis by line, along with the usual forms for permission and pictures." Carol uses the same language and implies that the number of chapters was the result of, not a predestination for, the substance of her thesis. She, too, "ended up with [emphasis added] seven chapters. They are, in order, (1) the introduction, (2) the review of the literature, (3) the methodology, (4) the emerging themes essential to the process..., (5) an educative inquiry..., (6) a constitutive response..., and (7) the concluding implications...."

I interpret the phrase "ending up" with any number of chapters to imply that the form originated from the nature of the research study itself, that is, from the interaction of the researcher with the context and with the analysis and interpretation of that context. This notion is congruent with the concept of emergent design so critical to qualitative research. Whether Pat and Carol know it explicitly or not, they describe the final form of their theses as a result of their efforts and not as an a priori structure they followed in order to document and legitimate their studies. The one anonymous correspondent in this study describes the formulation of the thesis format as follows:

> The contents [of my thesis] are organized according to principles of Chinese cosmology and numerology: 3 Parts, a focus on Chapter 5, nine chapters, and so on. The

organization sort of emerged appropriate to the content. My dissertation integrates materials from several disciplines, including geography, anthropology, folklore, history, botany, philosophy, and others; to comprehend the central idea, one has to peel it like an onion....

Similarly, my conceptual framework (perhaps a house made of sticks) seemed 'natural to me.' I didn't attempt to get the 'right answers' and may have speculated too much. My conclusion was really a handful of suggestions resulting from a mass of interrelated observations and insights I gained during the research process. Overall, writing the dissertation was a pleasant experience.

Nancy is another correspondent who did not use an a priori format. In addition, she suggests that personal background and graduate course work in qualitative research exercised their influence on the development of her thesis structure:

My dissertation has 6 chapters. I followed no format or guidelines beyond the useful suggestions of two key faculty members. I would guess that my dissertation is 'traditional' when compared to those in the humanities and the more qualitatively-oriented social sciences (e.g., cultural anthropology), but non-traditional when compared with dissertations in education and the more quantitatively-oriented social sciences (e.g., psychology)....

I would guess that my background...had a lot to do with how my dissertation project was conceived and carried out. I purposely did not look at any other dissertations before writing mine because I wanted mine to be original and, more importantly, to embody a form that was congruent with naturalistic inquiry.

Tradition's Influence

One of the notable discussion points on the topic of format is that other correspondents talked differently about what made sense to them. I am becoming convinced that for each novice qualitative researcher there was a developing sense of the project's coherence dictated by the project itself rather than any suggested a priori plan or structure. For example, Kathryn asserts that a traditional research format (e.g., Introduction/Problem—Literature Review—Methodology/Procedures—Analysis—Conclusions) made sense to her:

Why does my dissertation look the way it does? First off, yes, Kerlinger would recognize it. There are the typical five chapters. This was not dictated by my committee or any house rules. No other form made sense. I tried doing a more qualitative format but discarded it because it did not leave a sufficient 'paper trail' for anyone else to follow. Granted, it was initially hard to separate what needed to go into the Results chapter and what needed to go into Discussion, but the rule I developed was level of abstraction: that which appeared as cold, clinical description (how many said what) went into the Results section; that which was more story-like was included in the Discussion section. To reduce the boredom of qualitative data presented in this way and enhance believability, I used a lot of examples and quotes in Results, which was a lengthy chapter. It was not challenged in any way by my three quantitative committee members. In addition, I had quantitative data as well as qualitative. It did not make sense to do it any other way. I did not want to lose the sense of how interrelated were the two types of data. Although each type datum was derived from a different research question, the study would have been less meaningful if separated.

Other correspondents write that their theses retained a traditional chapter structure. Patricia's dissertation "is formatted along traditional lines with five chapters and appendices." Robert's dissertation also has five chapters. He writes, "I was influenced by traditional designs, but the presentation is unique. Chapter 4 presents the context in a lengthy narrative describing and capturing (I hope) the daily goings on at the site."

Throughout these descriptions, qualitative researchers reveal themselves to be conscious, interactive sensemakers. What makes sense to one may not make sense to another, but the choices and decisions made are grounded in the individual's perception of his or her focus and overall research purpose. I suggest that what may be important here is the idea with which I began the chapter: Qualitative researchers have to think about and decide for themselves many things that their colleagues who utilize an experimental design can take for granted. Perhaps, in the qualitative dissertation, the observable structure/format— the number of chapters, headings, inclusion and type of data, appendices, audit trails, and so on—provides the reader with an explicit clue to the researcher's processes of analysis and interpretation, which are a part of the meaning of the study. If this idea makes sense, then the notion of an "appropriate" format for qualitative dissertations probably does not exist unless it is explicitly linked to the substance/context of the study and the person and methodology that generated it. Marie comments on the emerging design of her thesis as well as her study:

> The chapter titles show how I drew on tradition and circumvented it:
>
> Chapter I.   Definition of the Problem
> Chapter II.   A Context for Inquiry (literature review)
> Chapter III.   The Emerging Design
> Chapter IV.   Overview: An Emerging Analysis
> Chapter V.   Refining the Analysis
> Chapter VI.   Two Case Studies
> Chapter VII.   Conclusions and Implications
>
> Like my study, then, my dissertation had an emergent design, and this was no accident. My goal was not to present reductive abstractions about what I myself had learned. It was to help others learn, to step readers —my participants and other researchers— through the learning/research processes I had gone through.

A traditional research format carries the comfort and burden of a set of assumptions about how to present the material in order that it might be more easily comprehended. What is not clear are the possibilities, only hinted at here, of alternative formats that would provide a more contextually grounded and interactive approach based on the given that the qualitative researcher is the human instrument. Does emergent design stop with the final reconceptualization of the study? I do not think so; as Marie suggested earlier, the presentation of her study required a format compatible with it. I must have believed this in the spring of 1986, when I wrote in the foreword of my thesis:

> Dear Reader:
>
> More and more dissertations which might be described as 'naturalistic' or 'qualitative' are being completed. This dissertation is an example of a naturalistic study in which qualitative methods were used. This terminology will be explained in Chapter I. However, I would first like to give you a preview of what to expect, as the format and style of this dissertation may be different from others you have read. (Meloy, 1986)

I am not trying to suggest that I was right all along. However, I now wonder whether the congruence of what we do and how we present it (the result of our implicit sense of the study's 'whole') is not as important to qualitative studies as the explicit structures that allow us to examine an experimental study. Does the format we choose somehow exemplify—rather than predetermine—the study?

Variations on a traditional dissertation reporting format will also require a greater degree of participation from the reader. Until recently, I do not believe readers of research have had to struggle (except with some statistical terminology) or become engaged with the reading material on a variety of levels in order to grasp the point. I think the concise nature of the impersonal research report has led us to expect 'good' research to be presented that way. Whether a priori or emergent, formats provide clues to the reader about the content and structure of ideas.

The correspondents cited so far appear to have had a great deal of say about the final format of their thesis. However, several others did not find that to be the case. Jean explains:

> I had to use the University's (Graduate School's) approved format: Chapter 1—Introduction; Chapter 2—Review of the Literature; Chapter 3—Methodology; Chapters 4 & 5—"The Body"; and Chapter 6—Conclusions (in my case Reflections and Implications). There was some pressure (which I resisted) to provide my committee with the first three chapters before they would consider accepting my study.
>
> The 'finished product' looks very much like a 'traditional' dissertation, although it is much longer than most. It is 406 pages —with 316 pages of actual text. There are seven separate appendices contributing 51 pages. I resisted the Graduate School's insistence that it should appear in two volumes, because I did not want it separated in any way for fear that continuity would be lost. My committee agreed with me. It appears in one HEAVY volume. It is not something you'd want to fall on your foot.

Although Jean seems to emphasize the size of her dissertation, at least two other issues seem salient to me. The first issue is that Jean argues for the continuity of her work, which I interpret to be compatible with the concept of the 'whole' under discussion. The second issue of interest to me is the presentation of the role of the graduate school in shaping dissertation decisions. The freedom, or lack thereof, of doctoral students to make decisions about their work has grabbed my attention, as indicated by the excerpt included here. I wonder how often this story is the case:

> Can I be facetious? My dissertation looks like this because that's the way my major professor wanted it to look. My advisor had the 'power'; I was only a VIP (very important peon) student, and I wanted to complete the thesis in a timely fashion. Seriously, all decision rules were reasonable decisions to which I had little trouble adhering.

> The final form of my dissertation is traditional, with one exception; it has 6 chapters instead of 5. I did a pilot study in order to sharpen my research skill. My committee wanted me to include the pilot study in the dissertation, although I did not use the findings for the final summary/ conclusions. I agreed, but stated to my major advisor that I wanted it to be in a separate chapter, to avoid confusing the reader. That was okay.

Gretchen suggests another possiblity where freedom of choice may be limited. She writes, "The general rule was that the format of the dissertation would be 'traditional'; justification was the potential for publication in academic journals. I accepted this with no problem, because I hoped for publication as soon as possible."

Summary

It seems, then, that qualitative dissertations look like they do for reasons that may or may not be integrally connected to the type of research undertaken. Institutional expectations, pleasing the dissertation committee, timeliness, and hopes for professional publication may mitigate against an emergent, nontraditional format. Kathy, who introduced my first presentation at the Qualitative Research in Education conference sponsored by the School of Education at the University of Georgia in 1989 and who became a correspondent in this study, writes about several of these concerns as well:

Jan. '91

> Dear Judy,

> When I returned home after your session at the Qualitative Research Conference, I wished I had gone home before lunch and not returned. I found the experience very unsettling. Many of the concerns and frustrations expressed were concerns of graduate students doing any type of dissertation....I regretted not making a comment about the uncertainty involved for both graduate students and major professors in working through a qualitative study. I think the uncertainty is as agonizing for major professors who care about research, their reputations and their students. Each study is different, and the questions that emerge need to be dealt with. It was argued that models do exist. They may not exist in all academic departments at all universities and colleges. And if they do exist not all of us are aware of what the models are. I have looked at a number of dissertations. My advisor has, too. There are things each of us like about

certain parts of each of the dissertations we have screened. Other dissertations have presented possibilities. None of them has served as a model for the case study I am writing....

I would like to know what the experts consider a model of a qualitative study. All of the qualitative dissertations I have read followed the five chapter quantitative format.

By outward appearances, some dissertations using qualitative research methodologies look like traditional, quantitative theses. From my experience with numerous doctoral students during the last 6 years, I am convinced that we have not clearly identified the possibilities and characteristics of communicating exemplary qualitative research. We have been focusing on how to do the research well, which is important. That we present it well and in a manner congruent with its purposes is not less important, although it has been less well explicated. Perhaps one reason this discussion has had difficulty gaining eminence is that aspects of the qualitative research process are inexorably intuitive and implicit—internal and integral to the human being as researcher—rather than rationally and explicitly standardized to be consistent across human beings. (See Wolcott, 1990, and Richardson, 1990, for their perspectives on this topic.)

As I was working with this material, several questions came to mind that might help students and faculty members alike to make appropriate decisions. "Appropriate" will be defined by your individual contexts. Although my predisposition is to suggest that a form congruent with the substance and methodology of a study enhances the ability of others to assess the integrity of the interaction of the researcher in context, the researcher as the human instrument, and the researcher as writer, there are several levels of questions that may facilitate long-range and immediate decision-making needs.

QUESTIONS

The first level questions have to do with realities that are most likely beyond a doctoral student's control; you may have to conform to them or be the first to argue!

1. The modal number of chapters in a dissertation is five; what is the norm at your institution?
2. How much control do the student, faculty members, and graduate school have in determining the appearance and style of the thesis? Which decisions, if any, are negotiable?
3. Do you know how much writing is involved? Are your committee members aware of how much reading is involved?
4. Is the goal of the dissertation to provide material for publication, or committee approval, or both? Are they different audiences? Are the respondents the intended audience? Do different audiences require different formats and styles? Different information? Whom will you please? Whom must you please?

Writing Issues

The questions seem to be headed toward consideration of individual writing style. If we focus on the format of the dissertation in terms of the number of chapters, it is clear that we still know very little about HOW the substance and style of the effort evolved into that particular format. Several of the correspondents offered vague clues into their process (e.g., the format "sort of emerged appropriate to the content" and "no other form made sense"). What is less vague is the concept that novice qualitative researchers are also making decisions as writers.

The Writing Sequence

Jane, who sent me regular updates during her dissertation research, describes the writing of her thesis this way:

> I sent [my advisor] partly completed drafts of chapters 1, 3, 4 and an outline of chapter 2 and some ideas for chapter 5. It was my intent to show the big picture of where I think the study is headed. My advisor appreciated that and said the way I was writing was intriguing—inside out, backwards and all over the place! I can't imagine working this kind of project any other way. I now have a much better sense of what exactly to include in my literature review, for example, and I really couldn't have known that until a great deal of findings were written up. Actually, it seems that the findings chapter (4) is in the best shape of all the chapters!! Because I now understand what the study is looking like, I can go back and refine the other chapters. I guess I have resisted accepting that kind of a process because it's so contrary to 'traditional' experimental designs! But it's really what has worked with me.

One reviewer of this book commented that the writing of traditional dissertations also follows the pattern that Jane suggests. Maybe so, but one of the things that captured my attention in Jane's description is the advisor's sense of intrigue: What is the level of understanding about a process such as Jane's, where the doing, reporting, analyzing, focusing, and writing do not combine or necessarily come together in a linear fashion? Does Jane's description explicate the characteristics of interaction among these processes in such a way that a sense of "intrigue" can be replaced with supportive acknowledgment of and for the processes? I think so. Jean's comments also provide support for the writing process:

> The last chapter I wrote was the methodology chapter. I wrote the chapters out of order—with the understanding and support of two writers with whom I was working. One of my respondents, who acted as my cheerleader, good friend and confidant, assured me at one point that all writers write what they can at the moment. I must say that the members of my committee came to understand my position and process. I wrote the conclusions before I wrote the balance of the 5th chapter.

> The "conclusions" are within the bodies of Chapters 4 and 5 and also in the final chapter. I do not like the word conclusions and did not wish to use it in my dissertation. My committee was comfortable with that.

Style Options and Requirements

Like format considerations, your writing style may be a matter of personal preference or an issue over which you have no control. My anonymous correspondent
chose to write "in third person, but only because it 'sounded right.'" Marie builds
a stronger case for her choices:

> I was a fairly good writer and quite analytical, which may have helped. I told my
> committee I was going to use a first person narrative and justified doing so using the
> social science literature I had discovered myself, quoting also from Don Graves, Paul
> Woodring and a few others who were calling for educational research to be written
> with a human voice. I stated that as my goal was to bring about change, I was going
> to write my research so that those individuals at the site could not only read it but also
> have enough of a vicarious sense of the methods I described writers using that they
> could imitate these methods if they chose. My department valued clear prose writing
> with a strong personal voice.

Like Marie, I was also able to make decisions about writing style. The decisions
were connected to a sense of how certain pieces of the dissertation needed to be
presented in order to support my conception of the 'whole':

> Chapter I introduces the study. The chapter is written in the third person, because the
> ideas incorporated in the thesis exist in the current literature of inquiry, organizations
> and education.
>
> Chapter II contains eight interview case reports. Each is written in narrative form in
> order to provide you with a sense of the interview interaction as it occurred. This
> chapter provides the data base from which Chapter III is derived....
>
> Chapter III is the final analysis of the interview data. This chapter is written in the
> first person, because it is my interpretations focused by the purposes of the study. I
> strongly urge you to refer to Chapter II and to your own sense of the eight case reports
> in order to determine the accuracy and/or possibility of the interpretations....
>
> Chapter IV presents four hypotheses about organizing....The thesis and the method-
> ology together generated the content from which the hypotheses are derived. (Meloy,
> 1986)

Some of us shared similar freedoms in our decision making; through this
research, I have found individuals who had concerns similar to my own. However,
there are also correspondents who chose qualitative research for their thesis
research who did not have as much freedom in their decision making. For example,
one of the correspondents remembers "tense" as a style and power issue:

> The biggest problem I had was writing in the past tense. My major professor wanted
> me to use past tense rather than present tense. During my first course, the professor
> insisted that students in the department write using the present tense. As a result, I
> relearned to write research papers using the present tense (for example, "Moore
> claims" rather than "Moore claimed".) I utilized this 'new writing technique' for 3

years. For my dissertation, my major professor required that I use past tense, stating
that some of the authors of my references were dead and that was about as past tense
as one can get. HA! HA! So of course, I used past tense!

Another correspondent's advisor also had the final say:

> My advisor was adamant about the need to use 3rd person and passive voice. I made
> a strong case for writing in a more interesting style, but my advisor found that too
> 'chatty' and insisted on an almost mechanical traditional research style. The resulting
> dissertation is a sure cure for insomnia.

Qualitative Researchers as Writers

I am convinced, given the reflections of my correspondents, the comments of
reviewers, and my own pursuits into the topic of writing and reading (Meloy, 1993)
that one characteristic of qualitative researchers is that they usually enjoy writing
and generally must be able to write well. Perhaps it is because of this characteristic
that the question of the "articulate I" as creator of fiction or presenter of fact remains
unresolved. Although qualitative researchers and scholars are continuing to define
and refine what qualitative researchers do, the resulting representations remain a
topic of debate—are they stories or research? (See Barone, 1992a, in press; Carter,
1993.) The point I wish to make here is simply that as a novice researcher, who by
necessity of the processes must be or will become a more able writer, you may also
need support for your writing choices. Jean is just one of the correspondents who
explicitly offers such support:

> My son just came in to tell me how easy I made writing look...writing does not come
> easily for me, although I think of myself as a writer and usually use a legal pad and
> pencil when I write, transferring my first draft to the computer—revising it then and
> then again, etc. I am composing this at the computer so I know it rambles and is not
> 'tight'. I face the terror of the blank page just like any other writer when I am supposed
> to be writing and the words don't flow.
>
> Actually I LOVE writing and look at the blank page as an invitation. One of the
> wonderful 'results' or 'conclusions' that I have taken away from the experience of
> writing a dissertation...is that I KNOW I am a member of the club of writers. Writers
> really are people. PEOPLE who write. I also feel a certain sense of accomplishment
> that NO ONE can take away from me.
>
> If I can do anything that will help others find their way as they struggle with a thesis
> or dissertation, I will be happy to do so. There were people there for me. Although
> you might face the blank page alone, you aren't really alone.

Jean is sincere in her offer; she continues to send me materials about reading
and writing. If you would like to write to her or any other of the correspondents,
addresses and additional information about them are located in Appendix B.

Figures

Only one correspondent mentioned developing figures for the thesis. I also struggled with the figures in mine, but the story given here is better:

> The figures created a huge <u>HEADACHE</u>. The ones within the second chapter were relatively easy to create. I am blessed with a wonderful husband who is a whiz on the computer. He used the computer facilities at work to create those figures for me. They looked as though they had been done by a professional draftsman. The other figures evolved. I was and still am extremely frustrated by the constraints put on figures by University Microfilms. Because I was doing original research neither my chair nor the 'chief nitpicker' at the Graduate School could offer much assistance. (I should be nicer about the person at the Graduate School responsible for dissertations. She was only doing her job. She is the person who uses a light table to look for type overs and a ruler to measure margins.) I learned—the hard way—to get absolutely everything in writing. I had all of the figures done and took them to the lady at the Graduate School who told me that they all had to be redone. I cried for hours over the cost and the time 'lost'.

Summary

Looking at the final form of qualitative dissertations will provide examples of the structures their authors used to organize their final sense of the research focus. The thesis may appear neat and tidy, but that final appearance seems to be an artifact of the research process rather than any a priori guidepost the researcher followed. This concept can be particularly troublesome for those of us who were taught to outline beginning with Roman numeral I. The processes of pulling together, sifting, organizing, and writing our thoughts are a challenge, because the coming together occurs in nonlinear, halting, and multiple ways. The task of choosing which strands to pursue, when to pursue them and how to pursue them, as well as how to organize them and write them up is a recurring and difficult one. As Paul Simon sings, "the nearer your destination the more you're slip-sliding away." I hope the preceding material provides a measure of comfort for the processes of researching and writing.

QUESTIONS

5. What is your writing style? Is your writing clear? Do others understand your writing? Do you like to write?
6. If your writing style just "seems right," what does that mean? Just right for what? Can you explain its sense to someone else? Do models exist to support your style preference? Are such efforts necessary to justify your own? Why or why not?

I would also like to pose several additional questions that come from my particular educational background and research experiences. I suspect the questions are grounded in my dissertation research experience, although until editing the final draft of this volume that idea was not even a conscious one; I had not included examples of my efforts in this book. I want to ask the following questions because I am trying to answer them for myself. I think the issue about why we do what we do and how we represent the resulting constructions is linked to the larger issue surrounding our choices to use qualitative or quantitative methodologies in our research.

QUESTIONS

7. Is qualitative research the result of a qualitative method? What makes a study qualitative? What assumptions are being made? How does anyone's writing reflect those assumptions?

8. Does writing reflect a quantitative or qualitative mind set? Is this important to consider? If methods are combined, can writing approaches be combined?

The excerpts from the correspondents' letters begin to illuminate the sense of not knowing what will happen until you get there. A major sensemaking strategy is ambiguity reduction (Weick, 1979). Qualitative researchers continuously make more and more, rather than fewer and fewer, decisions. It is only at the point of closure to a qualitative research experience (and even then there is most likely no singular billboard or flashing sign) that the complex, layered experience in which we engage begins to take shape as a sensible whole that can be—and indeed has been—organized, interpreted, and, perhaps, understood. Theses do not emerge all at once; if the thesis is qualitative, chances are it will not arrive head first. Understanding follows doing. However, as my correspondents suggest, the dissertation will indeed develop in a way congruent with perceived purposes, an understanding of methodological issues, and interaction with one's committee. In order to describe how such coherence comes about, the remaining chapters of this book are presented in a rough linear sequence in the order in which doctoral students might encounter them. Within this attempt at order, I also try to draw attention to the ongoing, multilayered sensemaking inherent in the role of qualitative researcher as the human research instrument. Although we can know more than one thing at one time, our ability to communicate multiple understandings simultaneously remains limited. I believe that this book can promote multiple understandings through the senses or connections it makes with you, the reader.

2

UNDERSTANDING AT THE BEGINNING:
Selecting and Working with a Committee

The singular probe I posed to my correspondents regarding their committees was: What did you have to negotiate with your committee? The correspondents wrote a great deal about this topic particularly as it relates to their expectations for their own work and the methodological expertise of faculty members. They generated numerous issues, including knowing your committee members, earning mutual respect, and recognizing expertise in qualitative and quantitative methodologies. They were also interested in the topics of faculty–student learning, the justification of qualitative approaches, and the frequency of committee–student interaction.

A Sense of Direction

Ann not only asserts knowledge of the faculty members she chose for her committee but also offers a clear sense of direction for own work:

> Three people made up my committee. My advisor's research interest made me want to attend the university I chose. One of the two other committee members was an individual with whom I had a two-year research assistantship. The third taught in my minor area, and I got to know this person, an anthropologist, through a course I took. I knew all three of these people respected the qualitative tradition in which I chose to work. Each have conducted or organized interview studies. All respected my research perspective.

The timing of and reasons for Patricia's committee selection appear to be different from Ann's. She writes, "I picked my graduate committee after I had begun my researches and selected both data gathering and analytical techniques. I point-blank asked potential committee members about any biases they had concerning qualitative approaches."

Jane asserts herself even more forcefully, stating, "I CHOSE A COMMITTEE FULLY COGNIZANT THAT I WANTED NOTHING BUT A QUALITATIVE

DESIGN; I ONLY ASKED FACULTY TO BE ON MY COMMITTEE WHOM I KNEW ENDORSED THE METHOD! (I guess that's clear....)"

Ann, Patricia, and Jane assert the importance of knowing the subject area and methodological predispositions of potential committee members. Jean must have believed that this was important, too, because she spends a good part of one letter describing her committee members. Among the many themes suggested in the following selection, I was interested in the number of ways the background and expertise of committee members can support a dissertation research experience:

> I'd like to give you a bit of background on my committee. I was able to select four members of my committee (my chair and three others). The fifth member of my committee was appointed by the Graduate School and was someone from outside of my department. That person's job is as the Graduate School's watchdog—to be sure that all procedures were followed to the letter of the law, "i's" dotted and "t's" crossed. That person may also contribute. The outside member is assigned on a rotating basis from a pool of all the members of the Graduate Faculty. He/she can be anyone.

> I did not know the man assigned, but his understanding of my subject matter and what I wanted to do was very helpful.

> My chair is a writer and edits a journal of qualitative research. He was kind and helpful and willing to admit he'd never done anything quite like what I was trying to do. I know I tried his patience more than once.

> Another committee member is my mentor and friend. We had worked as collaborators (and continue to do so). She understands my writing process and was able to help me 'cut and paste' in ways that my chair was not. Her chair had helped her through this writing experience, so she was able to pass the learning on to me. (I miss her being just down the hall. It is not easy collaborating with someone who is several hundred miles away. I must say that my phone bill has been a bit steep since my family's move.)

> Another committee member was a department chair. I had known this person as a teacher and friend. His research skills were invaluable; he protected me from myself and from another member of my committee when he felt that person's requests were out of line. He and another faculty member in my department (who is a GEM!) taught me how to use the phrase: "I am sorry but that is beyond the scope of my dissertation."

> Another faculty member was able to help me in many ways, because she had done her graduate work with an important researcher in my field. Finally, I also received a great deal of help from an anthropologist who teaches at the university. Because the materials I used were more like artifacts, her knowledge of anthropology and methodology were helpful.

Respect

Concomitant with knowing your own interests and the preferences/strengths of potential committee members is the issue of mutual respect and faculty confidence in your abilities. Several correspondents mentioned this issue explicitly. For example, my anonymous correspondent piqued my curiosity by writing, "What I had to negotiate with my committee was mainly my freedom of thought and action, which they were willing to give me once I had gained their confidence. Each of the five members of my committee were excellent and inspirational." I wrote back, asking for specific details on "gaining the confidence" of the committee. A brief time later, I received the following reply:

January 17, 1991

Dear Judith,

You have asked how I gained my committee's confidence, which I recommended as contributing to the success of my thesis experience. After entering graduate school, I observed early on that those PhD candidates least anxious about completing their theses were those with supportive and protective mentors, students who were also keeping close contacts with their other committee members and facilitating close contacts between them. I learned that these close and productive student–committee relationships are almost always initiated by students, and that everyone involved in the productive relationship had learned to respect one another. It is the task of the student to nurture the mutual respect that bears fruit (the thesis). It is most important for the student to demonstrate scholarly competence in small ways over a long period of time; for example, by undertaking independent studies with prospective committee members that require readings, research and a written report—and then, by attempting to get the research report published somewhere. This takes many semesters to accomplish, but with patience and luck students can earn the confidence of those faculty who will provide them ultimately with a positive thesis experience. When the time arrives to begin writing the thesis, the student may enjoy the unexpected freedom to act independently of close faculty supervision. This situation allows a student creativity in thesis preparation that otherwise might not be tolerated. This is only possible, of course, because of hard won committee confidence.

Maria, within a longer letter discussing the importance of a dissertation study group to her experience (see chapter 4), also wrote explicitly about respect:

As we [the Study Group] worked, we chose our committee members with care. My advisor and another of her colleagues, both of whom received degrees from the same university, were on my committee. I needed two other members and chose two faculty members (one in my program and one outside my program) whom I knew would be supportive of my efforts, because they respected me and my work. This may sound immodest, but members of the Study Group had already established their reputations as conscientious students who did quality work. We chose committee members who were willing to go along with our ideas (at least initially), because they respected us. We also picked committee members whom we thought would be intellectually open to the idea of qualitative research. It was not possible to have all committee members fit these criteria, because of the substance of some of the studies. We tried (and succeeded), however, to weight the committee membership with basically supportive faculty.

Faculty members have opportunities in class to make an impression on students. Making a solid impression on faculty members appears to be an equally important thing to do. Jean points out that an environment for interactions of mutual respect is also important:

> I believe that one of the strengths of the Center for Teaching and Learning's doctoral program...is its insistence that candidates select their own topics and their own committees (with the exception of the faculty member appointed by the Graduate School). Individual faculty members and members of the committee provide guidance. They challenge the candidate to consider possibilities; they offer articles, essays, and books, 'nudge' or 'nag' about deadlines, but avoid 'telling' the candidate what to do. They believe in self-directed learning and risk taking. They urge candidates to become actively involved in their own learning. They recognize that unless a candidate is self-directed and sees relevance in what is being studied, the learning won't be the same. They model and practice what they teach. There are hurdles that doctoral candidates must jump. A self-directed learner/risk taker jumps higher and more persistently.

The first set of questions in this chapter came to mind as I was thinking, "How fortunate some students and faculty members are!" Having specific interests or locating oneself at a particular university for particular purposes seems to be a 'smart' thing to do, especially because that was <u>not</u> indicative of my own thinking at the time.

QUESTIONS

1. Why did you choose to earn a doctorate? Will/do your reasons influence your choice of study, methodology, commitment? How much time are you willing to spend on this effort?
2. How did you select your university? Did you know what you wanted to do and with whom you wanted to work? Will the choices you have made support your dissertation research endeavor?
3. Do you know how doctoral students are viewed at your institution? In the department? Are they viewed as students? As co-learners? Does it matter to you?
4. What assumptions are you making about potential committee members? Have you read their work? Had a class with them? Heard about them? What do you need to know about them? How will you find out? What do they need to know about you? How will they find out?
5. Have you established a respectable track record of academic performance?
6. Can you assess the level of respect between you and the faculty members with whom you would like to work?
7. Do you have the sense that your faculty members are also learners? Do they have the sense that you are one?

Ambiguities

During doctoral study, the idealistic purposes of thinking and learning can give way to practical realities as individuals pursue their futures through their present day choices. Sometimes those choices are based on a priori knowledge and experience and sometimes they are not. What happens when: a student has only a general sense of his or her purposes and the next steps; the choice/availability of faculty members is limited; or, the student inadvertently ends up with a nonsupportive faculty member? One correspondent candidly admits:

> If I am to be honest, the committee was formed with little real understanding of the consequences which would result from individual selection.
>
> My department had only recently developed a PhD program and two committee members were a 'given', the department chairman and the Dean of the School of Education. The department chairperson was no problem, while the Dean was a 'quant' to the extreme, often remarking how the dissertation had to be 'formal' and 'real research' (different from my approach).

Qualitative/Quantitative

The quantitative/qualitative aspects of committee selection are also a source of ambiguity. Gretchen recalls.

> Graduate committees must come in all combinations of expertise. I had no quantitative 'experts' on mine, although three of the four members had done some quantitative studies. My dissertation director encouraged a qualitative approach with triangulation provided by also including quantitative tables (more about that later). Other committee members included the faculty member who teaches field research methods, a specialist in my subject area and the 'outside' person who was actually the most helpful of all, because he taught evaluation using Guba and Lincoln (1981) as the course textbook.
>
> I now wish that I had included someone who was expert in quantitative studies as a part of my committee. I have had to redo all the statistical analyses to meet the requirements of journal reviewers; what my committee accepted is not accepted by others.

Gretchen's comments provide a clear example of how many issues of concern to doctoral students intermingle. In order to stay with the immediate topic, two correspondents offer the following suggestions to those of you less clear about the implications of your methodological choices. Lew suggests, "Talk to (screen) potential committee members. As a student, you may not understand the gap between qualitative and quantitative; talking to faculty members about what you might want to do will help." Tim adds, "My experience with quantitative-positivist oriented professors has been pretty good.... Quantitative researchers are not ignorant or inherently evil. Students should appeal to their intellectual curiosity."

Summary

In the case of my own dissertation, my methodological background was well established by the time I was ready to prepare and defend the proposal and select the final committee. Having taken a full load of research courses—a seemingly endless sequence of statistics and design courses, qualitative inquiry courses, and courses on theory building and evaluation—I was able to "appeal" to at least one quantitatively oriented professor in part because I could explain the differences between what I proposed to do and how a study using an a priori framework would vary from that. Although I believe that qualitative research stands on its own merits, I felt it was necessary for me to ground my methodological choice in a solid understanding of the options available. I think that mutual respect can be earned by being able to speak the same language and then to argue effectively for the strengths of one's choices. Kathy is just one of the correspondents who also thought about this issue:

> Many committee chairs are learning about qualitative dissertations along with their students as they make collaborative decisions. The research experience and background of each of these people and the relationship they have developed during the time the student was in the graduate program affect decisions made. Sometimes there is a common knowledge base; sometimes there isn't. The student at yesterday's session who is working with her third major professor is one extreme. Students who have done research collaboratively throughout their doctoral program are at the other. Some of us get feedback and input from other committee members. Others do not. The process can be an emotional one for both the student and the professor.

QUESTIONS

8. What are the local guidelines/requirements, if any, for selecting a committee? What would be the pluses and minuses of any one particular faculty member? Topic? Methodology? What is worth it to you?
9. Are there people in your department or college who can support your committee-member selection?
10. How many committee members must you have? Is the committee for the proposal the same one for the thesis? Who 'picks' the outside committee member? Are there any Graduate School requirements? Department requirements?
11. Does the environment in your department, college, or university support qualitative research? Do you know where qualitative research expertise is the norm?
12. What are the pluses and minuses of having a quantitative researcher on your committee? What (whom?) do you need to be 'successful' as you define it? When is a critic useful? What kinds of criticism can you take? Can you define the kind of help you need? Do you know which kind of support any individual faculty member may or may not be able to give?

Faculty–Student Learning

Whether there is a "quant" on a committee seems less essential than whether a student is able to work with others, both students and faculty members, who are knowledgeable. If Kathy is correct in her earlier summary excerpt, then the range in the levels of knowledge and the ability to support graduate student efforts vary from individual to individual, institution to institution. More important than the variability, perhaps, are some examples of what is being done about it. In an excerpt from a lengthy first letter, Maria describes the interactive learning that can occur among students and faculty and how a mutual faculty–student learning environment supports a graduate student's possibilities for doing a solid piece of research:

> One of the things that fascinated me about the experience of the Study Group was the learning that occurred among faculty. I was the first member of the Group to defend my overview and dissertation. I perceived that during both meetings, my advisor played a 'teaching' role with the two 'outside' committee members. I don't mean by this that he defended my work for me, but rather, he placed my work within the larger context of interpretive research. At strategic moments, he stepped in and gave the other committee members the language they needed to discuss my dissertation within the interpretive paradigm. He modeled for them what were appropriate questions. When they asked questions out of the positivist paradigm, he would reframe them in a way that was more consistent with the interpretive paradigm. I believe he was able to do this, because of his personal style and the respect/stature he had with the other committee members. Now, here's what is fascinating to me. During my defense, one member of my committee asked questions that were not appropriate to the interpretive paradigm. He subsequently served on the committees of other study group members. As he participated in later meetings, he was the one who began to 'correct' other faculty who were asking inappropriate questions. In short, he learned from my advisor and the members of the Study Group and then began educating other faculty. We saw this happen with several other faculty within our program who served on more than one of our committees....
>
> As we went along, not only the faculty/committee members were learning. So were we. We learned from each other what questions to anticipate and how to articulate the rationale for what we were doing. The success of our learning was demonstrated, I believe, by the fact that several Study Group members did not have to make a single revision in their final documents. They were able to present the research method, rationale and results with such clarity and precision, committees accepted the dissertations as written.

Robert recalls his experience around student–committee learning this way:

> Your questions in the area of analysis reminded me of how important it was to educate my committee. They learned about emergent hypotheses, categories, field methods, grounded theory and other concepts and jargon the qualitative researcher lives with daily. As long as I appeared to have a grasp on the methods, the committee was satisfied with the analysis. (I found I was my harshest critic in this area. Although I

was satisfied that the methods were good and that themes were emerging, I kept an abiding/nagging feeling that what I observed was prejudiced by biases I was unable to account for. In essence, I questioned my own integrity....)

The only point I had to negotiate with the committee was the 'so what.' I was required to convince them that the exercise was as important as the results. Since my study was the first of its kind to be undertaken at my university, it was critical that my blueprint was readable—that this was as important as the conclusions that emerged proved challenging.[1]

In the following excerpt, Pat describes how she and her committee began to learn about qualitative research. Her experience is unlike any other of the correspondents. I am impressed that a university would provide the opportunity she describes. I also realize it will be a while longer before qualitative researchers are the norm at institutions of higher education:

My department did not know what or which way would be the most appropriate for a non-traditional dissertation. Outside experts from the University of Florida and the University of Tennessee were brought to the campus to lecture and conduct individual research appointments. The department chairperson or my committee chairperson was present at these appointments. My dissertation was developed through individual research appointments. At the first appointment, Rodman Webb from Florida State approved of the research project. At the 2nd appointment, Kathleen Bennett from the University of Tennessee made format suggestions which resulted in the chapter layout for my dissertation. I took her suggestions because they made sense to me.

Justifying Qualitative Research

"Educating the committee" can be a real life experience for neophyte qualitative researchers. Several correspondents honed in on the lack of a shared tradition and the feeling that they had to justify any alternative approach. Patricia, perhaps unknowingly, makes the latter issue explicit, saying, "I was fortunate in having a dissertation advisor who had had a number of his students working with qualitative formats. His own work is often done in a qualitative mode, and thus, he has significant experience in justifying the legitimacy of these approaches." Carol mentions the issue as well, writing, "I graduated May, 1989, and used qualitative

---

[1]At this time, I want to offer an aside about the writing and reading of this book. After deciding it would not be enough to simply offer a book of letters (in other words, acknowledging that I undertook the research with some purpose in mind), a major frustration became the selecting and placement of particular letters and excerpts within the book. Each excerpt, no matter how focused the author seemed to be, usually contains more than one idea or issue (e.g., Robert's excerpt just given, or Gretchen's, p. 17). One characteristic that I believe qualitative researchers share, as Robert suggests, is the almost constant questioning of their choices. Decision making is a process that constantly refines/defines our 'product'. I know I said that this was not a book of imperatives, but if I may offer one, then it is that you do not let the choices I make stop you from discovering and discussing other issues of importance to you.

research to do my dissertation. In particular, I used phenomenological investigation as the method....Those of us who use it must defend it; however, the quantitative folks still have the upper hand!" Ann's interaction with her advisor illuminates the concern more directly:

> I did have a strong and supportive adviser who pushed me through, although I found the process a painful one. She said to me when I saw her in January, after she had read someone's completed dissertation with a long section justifying qualitative research, "Why do you all feel so guilty about qualitative research?" I'm not really sure why, but I think we are continually squaring ourselves with science and not just our committee.

Something is still going on 'out there'; even for recent doctoral recipients there remains a sense that things have to be justified, excused, or explained again. Jean expresses a similar notion:

> Is qualitative research getting a 'bad rap' because it is viewed as easy? I think that it is somehow viewed as not as rigorous, because it does not involve statistics and all of the mumbo jumbo that goes with extensive statistical analysis. There seems to be a mystique that surrounds and over-values anything scientific and/or mathematical. One of the doctoral students in geology asked me—while I was a doctoral student—if I had to meet the same requirements to receive a Ph.D. that she did. She was amazed to discover that we had to meet the same requirements. She was surprised to learn that I had to conduct original, creative research for my dissertation and that I had to develop my own topic, etc.

If some doctoral students feel defensive about their decision to undertake qualitative research, then might it be less from the fact of their methodological choices per se than it is from the fact that they are inexperienced researchers and methodologists, less able to explain and argue their choices and less sure about knowing what they are doing and why? Tim offers several suggestions that make sense to me:

> Have a concrete idea about what qualitative research means to you. Until you are confident in your understanding of what you are going to do and how you are going to do it, you will never be certain if you are conducting the research properly. Many of my colleagues at your workshop seemed uncertain about what qualitative research was. Until they know this, they will be lost, both in explaining their work to others and in conducting the research for themselves.

> Stress the importance of knowing both sides of the paradigm dialogue. Although Dr. Wolcott said qualitative researchers no longer needed to defend their paradigm in addition to their research in theses and dissertations, he is speaking from an educational research perspective, where qualitative research is more accepted. Students should know the assumptions of both the qualitative and quantitative perspectives to better define and defend their own work. As long as their work is under the evaluative control of researchers unsympathetic to qualitative research, qualitative researchers

will have to defend their perspective as a whole, if only to place their own work in context for their reviewers.

Harry Wolcott, who was a keynote speaker at the 1991 Georgia conference and offered many pointers to all who attended, suggests the following in his 1990 book *Writing Up Qualitative Research:*

> ...In the last two decades, qualitative methods—which in many instances would be portrayed more accurately as qualitative techniques—have come to be widely known and accepted. There is no longer a call for each researcher to discover and defend them anew, nor a need to provide an exhaustive review of the literature about such standard procedures as participant observation and interviewing....Neophyte researchers who only recently have experienced these approaches firsthand need to recognize that their audiences probably do not share a comparable sense of excitement about hearing them described once again. (p. 26)

Although Professor Wolcott's perspective may be correct from his point of view and for certain people in certain places, the correspondents' reflections continue to focus attention on the fact that the language, assumptions, practice, and products of qualitative research are neither common nor necessarily commonly accepted at our colleges and universities, or between faculty members and graduate students. One question I have about this is: Even if methodologies and strategies become 'common' from a faculty member's point of view, aren't doctoral students—regardless of methodological perspective—expected to be able to defend their choices about <u>any</u> "such standard procedures"? I recall graduate school stories about individuals who did not do well at their final dissertation defense because they could not explain in-depth the choices surrounding their research designs, which were slightly complicated statistical analyses done by or with someone from another department who <u>understood</u> statistics. Perhaps, as Professor Wolcott suggests, an "exhaustive review of the literature" is not as necessary as some other means—within the thesis or at the defense—of determining a student's understanding of his or her choices?

Fortunately, several of my correspondents wrote about this issue from two perspectives—as doctoral students and then more recently as junior faculty members:

Dear Judith,

I am currently working with an honors student. As I talked with her in an attempt to have her define her project for me, it became apparent to both of us that qualitative methods would address her questions and purposes. As it has turned out, it would have been easier if her questions and purposes could have been addressed quantitatively. I could have located a site for her and been able to bow out quietly and quickly with my obligations fulfilled. As it is, I have become her advisor and first reader, although I am not on the Honors Committee. I am stepping on all sorts of toes. The 'official' Honors Committee members are NOT qualitative researchers; they have no interest in qualitative research and view it with suspicion. Because of their lack of interest and time, they have allowed me to assume the role I have. I find myself defending all I believe and do. It seems to be taking a tremendous amount of time. It is also forcing me to further clarify my thinking.... I really am enjoying my work with her and learning a great deal.

These people do not understand qualitative research; they do not seem to understand the role that a researcher's purposes and questions have in determining the approach used. They do not seem to grasp the emergent nature of qualitative research or writing as a discovery process (some of the wonderful moments of "AHA" that my honors student has experienced have come as she has begun to write).

A story from a second correspondent is more harsh:

I have to contrast my graduate experience with that of the students at the university I came to (and have since left). While my graduate institution was very strong...this place was a great contrast; it shows up in the way doctoral research is rigidified there.

When I first arrived, I had a doctoral student who had been given a rigid quantitative format in a research course. She said she 'had to follow' this format when writing her prospectus, even though I was her dissertation director. I also sat in on a prospectus defense in which I was interested. I watched aghast as two quantitatively trained committee members gutted the heart of the study, stating that the questions posed were not legitimate. No one on her committee came to her defense, although her topic was well thought out and her methods were carefully planned.

I have also spent a good bit of time helping other people's advisees who have received permission to do qualitative theses but were forced to take the quantitative research sequence and then left entirely on their own to pick up the research knowledge they would need. Sadly, it gets worse. They struggled with committees, often for political reasons, that had no member knowledgeable in qualitative methods. Their studies were shaped and reshaped by the competing whims of those who understand less than they about what they were doing and about the assumptions and methods they used. Unfortunately, the students with whom I talked did what they were told, some knowing, some not, that it was indefensible.

I've heard that the politics on some committees were horrible, that with one exception, quantitative researchers serving as advisors rarely defer to the (mostly junior) committee members who were well versed in qualitative approaches.

I believe that the experience of one other correspondent needs to be mentioned here:

My advisor kept tacking on additional quantitative 'items' such as a self-report questionnaire for our subjects, to be subjected to multivariate analysis. The comment was, "You won't have to include this in your dissertation, but gather the information while you can. Then use it later for convention papers or articles." Later, I was told to include everything in the dissertation.

Themes mentioned earlier, such as mutual respect and faculty-student learning, are only two of the issues emerging again from these anecdotes, although from a different perspective. A colleague of mine offers yet another viewpoint here, when he quite fortuitously (for my purposes) wrote seeking feedback on a proposal for the 1993 AERA conference:

> I am known in my college as the person who does qualitative research. Just as everyone always wanted a statistician on his or her committee, now I'm in great demand. Qualitative research methods became the new mysterious wand that one waves over data to make them kosher. For other faculty, there is little recognition or ownership of the possibility that we are engaged in inquiries of greater meaning. Questions about reliability and generalization take up the majority of an oral examination. The students seem to glimpse the sense of having done valuable research for themselves but are easily cowed into believing that the year's work they have completed is really better described as 'exploratory research'. My position as a methodologist often feels like that of a fall guy. The statisticians seemed more like priests (or rabbis, thinking of my kosher metaphor), but the faults faculty find in the dissertations seem to directly reflect on the intrinsic inadequacy of the methods—for which I am clearly responsible or irresponsible, depending how deep is the annoyance with these new-fangled methods.

Summary

Experience tells me that the qualitative–quantitative arguments have filtered down from the lofty level of articulate debate to the concrete level of implications for practice. When it comes to practice, novice researchers and faculty members who are less knowledgeable about qualitative research do not seem always to be working hand-in-hand to insure a process and product of explicit, well-honed, and arguable integrity and thereby intrinsic value—even if the results are not statistically significant. The inherent power inequality between student and faculty member and/or new faculty member and tenured faculty member can shape theses research efforts in direct and significant ways. The power dynamic is undoubtedly problematic to the future of qualitative research, because the dissertation experience often sets the tone and establishes the template for future researchers and research. In order to consider the best research practice using any methodology, I believe that a few questions have been raised that must be addressed. I am sure that there are other questions as well.

QUESTIONS

13. What is your current level of experience and knowledge of research methodologies/methods and practice? Will your level of knowledge make a difference in what you choose to do? Should it?
14. As student or faculty member, have you gotten the education you need to do your job well, that is, do you know your stuff?
15. What does an experienced faculty member need to know to support students who choose to do qualitative research for their dissertations? What are the

current 'norms' of accepted practice, such as those mentioned by Wolcott? Should a student have to defend them?

16. What is the political environment at your university, college, or in your department regarding qualitative research? Will political, personal, or publication issues influence your methodological decision making? The appearance of your dissertation?

17. How willing are you to experience self-doubt, to not know exactly what you are doing? How interested are you in figuring things out? Is qualitative research for you?

18. If your department is qualitative 'resource' shy, what alternatives are available to support doing qualitative research?

19. Who will 'control' which data are collected? What types of suggestions are reasonable? Based on which criteria? What jeopardizes the rigor/integrity of any type of study? Do you know?

20. Can you choose your compromises, that is, what are you willing to negotiate and what will you remain firm about? Is it important to know "what qualitative research means to you" or what qualitative research means?

21. What is the reality for qualitative researchers once they have completed their doctorates? Which, if any, responsibilities will your newly acquired knowledge base require of you? Do you think the dissertation will be the last piece of research you will ever do? (If you believe your thesis IS the last piece of research you will ever do, please write and tell me what you are thinking, c/o P.O. Box 187, Poultney, VT 05764. Thanks.)

22. Will/are new faculty members able to influence the status quo? Are they available to answer your questions? Can you answer theirs? How many students are they working with?

Committee–Student Interaction

The level of involvement an individual seeks throughout the dissertation experience depends on individual strengths, needs, and context. Some will operate almost independently; others work more closely with their committees. Certain committees and/or advisors may want the doctoral students to work on their own, whereas others may want frequent opportunity for feedback. Students may prefer a lot of feedback or choose to work alone until the material appears to be reasonably cogent. Tim agrees, along with several other correspondents, that frequent contact with committee members is "crucial":

> When dealing with committee members I believe it is crucial to be in constant contact—work with them, show them what you are doing, make certain they are with you from the beginning.... Without such guidance, I would feel lost. More importantly, I would be setting myself up for some potential surprises when the thesis is submitted if I did not know the opinions and questions of my committee members throughout the research and writing period.

Jane's following comments remind me that not everyone experiences similar circumstances. She says, "It's also significant to tell you that I live 500 miles from my chair! I am unable to run to my chair with lots of little questions! Mostly I just solve them!" Another correspondent importantly complicates the issue of the frequency of interaction between committee and student:

> In my case, it was not geography alone that determined contact. I knew my dissertation advisor would be my biggest hurdle, so I sent draft copies. Only after numerous (and I do mean numerous) rewrites and when the dissertation was 75% done, did I solicit feedback from other committee members. Also, I never shared only one chapter with my advisor; I sent several chapters at once, because my advisor needed to see how my ideas were developing across the whole dissertation.

The choices you make around this issue will be influenced by your particular needs and the types of efforts—from yourself and your committee members—you believe will support your work. Kathy, who was reflecting about writing, offers a few additional concerns:

> Everyone on my committee has encouraged writing in the first person from the beginning, but I interpreted their expectations to include expository rather than narrative writing. I got hung up with my perceptions of the expectations of the committee members who would be reading the study. At one point, I wanted to be told what to include and how to write it and was willing to give up my own voice, a voice expressed through style and content and the freedom to try it out my way. It was not until I felt that I was deadlocked and totally unsure of the expectations of others and decided to finish without any other advice or criticism and then let people react, that I discovered my own voice, a voice that was reflected in a more confident writing style, my writing style. Prior drafts had been written with individual faculty members as the intended audience and were influenced by other studies considered as possible models.

Kathy is not alone in her feeling of wishing that the proverbial "someone" would just tell her what to do. Jane concurs:

> It occurred to me that I have been conditioned—all through my schooling and even now in graduate school—to think that the teachers/professors had THE ANSWERS. Even now I have been tempted to want my chair to tell me THE WAY to do it. Old habits die hard...! I keep reminding myself that there is not just ONE WAY, obviously a view inherent in qualitative research. I also realize that completing a dissertation is in part an exercise in learning to make decisions and trust one's own judgment.

Unlike the guideposts available for quantitative research, the latitude for individual decision making—indeed the myriad of choices—can be daunting for the novice qualitative researcher.

QUESTIONS

23. What amount, kind, and frequency of interaction does your committee expect? What do you expect? Who will initiate the contact?
24. Does your chair wish you to share your writing with all committee members from the very beginning or after he or she has the opportunity to provide some initial feedback?
25. How much feedback do you personally need? How much can you handle?
26. Will it matter which chapters you solicit for feedback first? Why or why not?

Student–committee interaction appears to be the important vehicle for a successful thesis experience. There are obviously challenges and possibilities within the circumstances of individual experience. The intent of this chapter is not only to highlight some concerns, but also to suggest possible ways of thinking about issues integral to the selecting of and interacting with a doctoral committee. Knowing each other, working with mutual respect, and co-learning appear to be actions supportive of a positive dissertation research experience—quantitative or qualitative. However, uncertainty about committee expectations as well the implications of methodological choices and institutional protocol can create both mental and emotional friction.

3

UNDERSTANDING BY PROPOSING:
Preparing and Defending the Proposal/Prospectus

The first piece of official writing usually shared with a committee is the dissertation proposal. The correspondents' letters provide evidence of a variety of learning cultures as they describe how the correspondents prepared the proposal and what they assumed and learned by doing it. The letters also reveal some concerns that only became apparent to the correspondents after the defense and acceptance of the proposal, when data collection and analysis were in progress. Pulling the prospectus together for presentation, however, is the first step.

Proposal Presentations

The following excerpts highlight the difficulties that two correspondents experienced as they were 'learning by doing'. Carol recalls:

> When I first wrote up the proposal, etc., I outlined the dissertation in a traditional quantitative way (problem, literature search, methodology, findings, conclusions). My committee laughed me out of the building. They let me know that qualitative research is different. It was okay to talk in the first person! And 'real' qualitative research does not know what the thesis is until the interviews are done and analyzed.

Another correspondent also found the first proposal presentation to be less than successful:

> My first field study proposal was rejected flat by my advisor. It took another six months to enrich the original plan. The resulting study was much better.
>
> The addition of a priori hypotheses about demographic differences was something 'tacked on' by my advisor at the last minute before the proposal was signed...more with the view of providing publishable data than from a philosophical basis.

Still another correspondent offers some additional detail around the effort of developing and presenting the prospectus.

> After I decided on the topic for my dissertation, I spent several months reading the literature trying to find a theory or framework by which to interpret what I thought I might find(!) I put together a short proposal and distributed it to committee members. My chair does qualitative research, but of a more theoretical or secondary analysis bent. My chair was supportive of my approach and objectives in this first proposal, which involved testing a series of hypotheses.... Another committee member, also of a qualitative orientation and who I think was very wise, said "If this is what you really want to do, fine, I'll support it, but I think you'd have a better study if you took a more inductive approach...." Another committee member, who is a seasoned field researcher, said the same thing: "Just go and start hanging out in the setting and talk to everyone about everything and write down everything you observe and see what emerges as interesting. Don't worry about having an analytical framework at this point." (quotes are not their exact words, but a paraphrase).

> So this is what I ended up doing, and I think it was an excellent decision. That is, I ended up approaching the study much more inductively, with justification provided by sociologists Glaser and Strauss (1967) in their volume *The Discovery of Grounded Theory*. This is an excellent but densely written manifesto....Schooled as I am in the deductive method, I had some resistance to this approach (as well as emotional anxiety as to 'but what if nothing interesting appears?'), but of course it has, and I think my project will be much richer for having proceeded this way. As it turns out, the focus is....

The reflections just given suggest some of the struggles past experience and unclear expectations foster as doctoral students begin to undertake a qualitative research project. What makes me smile is the beginning of the final sentence in the last excerpt, "As it turns out..." has the familiar ring of several statements made earlier, for example, "I ended up with." The foci of qualitative research proposals emerge as a result of interaction in the research context; a priori ideas give way to issues discovered there. Although novice qualitative researchers are told that research foci "emerge," the aforementioned excerpt suggests how changes in preparation and thinking enabled a particular focus to do so.

Proposal Models

Course work, as well as committee member suggestions, can support the writing of the prospectus. Ann recalls:

> When I wrote my (1st) proposal, I was in a research methodology class. As well as preparing the class for the qualifying exam, the instructor required us to write a proposal. In each class we presented our efforts toward finding a question, preparing the method and planning the literature review. To stop those questions, "What does a

proposal look like?" and "How do I write one?" the professor distributed former students' successful proposals.

The proposal I subsequently completed was modelled on these successful proposals, with a similar skeleton of statement of purpose, literature review, methods, analysis section and chapter outline of the dissertation. Only up to a point were these samples proposals helpful, however. As I understood my question better, I found that writing a proposal was a creative process—it became my proposal and no one else's.

At the beginning, but not during the writing I found books such as Yin's (1984) helpful. It was too prescriptive later when I was well away into creating my proposal. After I finished my proposal and before the defense, I found the books helpful to tighten certain sections (methodology and analysis) and to just generally prepare for the defense of the proposal.

I made it clear that my research question was well-grounded and of both practical and theoretical significance. I also tried to emphasize that my study was exploratory; my sample would be drawn....

Although no hypotheses were written into my proposal, I did find it helpful on my own to prepare a long list of hypotheses after I had conducted my pretest of the interview questions. I compiled this list partly because so many thoughts and speculations came out of those preliminary interviews and analysis, and because I thought they might help guide and shape later analysis after data collection.

One of the themes that both interests and simultaneously troubles me is the variety of ways the correspondents talk about qualitative research. Because of my education and subsequent understanding of qualitative research, words like "subjects" and "hypothesis" make me nervous. What I have noticed throughout all of the letters from the correspondents is that our learning around qualitative issues has not been common; there are ways in which we are not all thinking and doing the same things. Although I am by no means certain that we must, I sense that the excitement of doing qualitative research at this time is dampened for many who have concerns about what we do and how we are doing it. Paula offers a more explicit description of one of her concerns:

One thing that is in my journal is the question of whether I should call my study 'qualitative research' or 'naturalistic inquiry'. Isn't there a quote out of Shakespeare, "What's in a name?" I felt that if I could put a name on the kind of research, then I would know better what rules to follow. I think these terms need to be better defined for students. Are they the same? I am not a qualitative researcher; at the time, I was a student trying to complete a dissertation. Maybe researchers know the differences among terms, but I don't. The literature which I read did not deal very well with this issue, although some of the authors tried to handle it. Let's define some terms for students and for faculty who are used to working with quantitative studies.

I think it makes sense to highlight this concern here, because the proposal process is at the beginning of the formal dissertation research experience. Most doctoral students are novice researchers; what they learn and begin to understand conceptually through their course work takes on additional and more concrete meaning in practice. Perhaps the time for the defense of a 'qualitative' proposal ought to be later in the research process, after an initial investigation has been undertaken around a focusing idea. As several correspondents have already suggested, the selection of the committee and the clarification of the proposal came <u>after</u> they had spent some time in the research context, that is, after they had begun figuring out the rules.

Summary

Proposal writing does not appear to be something that comes naturally. We learn not only by example but also by the reactions and suggestions of committee members. The correspondents remember having a tentative sense about what to do and how to do it. Preparing a proposal that can be successfully defended (substantively and methodologically) is one area that clear guidelines and examples can support.

QUESTIONS

1. What does a proposal look like? How might one that incorporates qualitative research methodologies differ from other models? Should it differ?
2. What is the role of theory in qualitative research? Are a priori theoretical frameworks and quantitative hypotheses compatible with your understanding/knowledge/definition of qualitative research? How so? If not, why not?
3. Is it possible for a student to have an idea of what he or she wants to do but have no clear sense about how to get at it? Is this much ambiguity troublesome?
4. What do you believe your committee members' roles to be? What do they believe their roles are? Have you discussed this topic with them?
5. Who is going to tell whom about what you are going to do? How much guidance do you expect? How much responsibility are you willing to take?
6. What does it mean to "create" a proposal? Where is the latitude and where are the constraints?

More About Proposing

Ambiguity

One question for faculty members that may be crucial is this: If we are in the position to tell students what to do (or accept what they suggest), then what are the implications for student research based on our knowledge or lack thereof? If we add the newness for the student of writing a proposal to the simultaneous newness of trying to figure out the ramifications of qualitative research, the sum is a certain amount of additional ambiguity within committee–student interactions.

Several correspondents suggest that understanding what we are doing while distinguishing or justifying the qualitative from the quantitative remains an issue. Although this volume is presented in a somewhat linear form across dissertation checkpoints, almost every excerpt contains more than one idea that would fit under more than one heading. The concept of "mutual simultaneous shaping" discussed by Lincoln and Guba (1985) appears to be an appropriate descriptor for the interactive processes and concurrent ambiguity that the human being, as research instrument, experiences. Maria remarks on the difficulties posed by such ambiguity during the proposal defense:

> One of the difficulties in writing a proposal for interpretive research is the uncertainty surrounding the format and content of the results. We found it difficult to maintain the integrity of the inductive research process and still answer committee members' questions about our anticipated results....As we gained more experience in writing overviews, we became more skillful in articulating the process that would lead to the final construal. My advisor also encouraged people to do pilot studies to collect some preliminary data so they could begin to get a sense of what the construal might be.

> One of the needs I had in developing both my proposal and dissertation was to articulate a rationale for what I was doing— essentially building an argument for the legitimacy of my research design....My intent was to show that grounded theory was, in its way, as rigorous as more traditional research methods.

Kathy recalls how ambiguity 'feels' when she describes preparing her proposal:

> Dear Judy,

> I wished someone would have told me how to write a proposal to do a qualitative study in a school district. I followed the guidelines dictated by the Graduate School and modeled my request on that of a colleague who did a case study in one school.

> I did not consider the uncertain nature of the project I was studying or the fact that the continuous process of evaluation and revision would affect the choice of participants I would want to interview. I did not include unknown possibilities when I wrote my proposal. It seemed fine at the time to me and to my committee members.

In a subsequent letter, she reiterates:

> I told you during one of our conversations that I would have welcomed guidance when writing my proposal and especially with my request to do research in the school system. I wish I had been advised to make the proposal open ended enough to allow for the changes that take place when doing a qualitative study. I would have liked to have interviewed more people as the study evolved.

> I never considered writing an amendment to the request that had been approved by the university and the school district. I wish now that I would have pursued that. I raised many more questions than I answered.

Paula shares Kathy's concern:

> I 'walked' a careful line between keeping within the guidelines of my proposal and being able to 'move with the groove' so that I could change plans/tactics as needed. I didn't understand how much latitude I had or would be allowed to use. If I moved too far from my proposal, would I have to get my committee's approval? Would I have to go to the Internal Review Board?

Ann did not face this problem and writes:

> My committee did believe in some flexibility in the proposal—if you need to keep interviewing, go ahead, one said. I simultaneously worried that 30 persons were too many and not enough. I now think, having collected the data, that 30 is just right. I believe I've reached the saturation point in terms of findings that Bogdan and Biklen (1982) speak of.

Kathy raises an additional issue about the implications of an emergent design for the proposal:

> During your workshop, I reacted negatively to the suggestion that students should submit an outline of chapter headings and sub-headings, including an estimated length under each, at the onset of the study. Again, I think uncertainty is characteristic of many of our studies. Headings and organizational structure often develop during the process of data collection and analysis. I could not have written an outline of my case study when I defended my proposal that looked like the nine chapter document that has resulted from my study. I do believe that decisions about the general format need to be established in advance: where the review of literature fits, if the methodology used is described in a separate chapter, whether discussion of the findings is ongoing or a separate part of the report.

QUESTIONS

7. Will you be able to anticipate the 'results' of your study? Should you? Could a pilot study, or preliminary hours in context, enable you to refine your focus? Anticipate results? Would you do this before your proposal defense?
8. Is your proposal open ended enough to enable changes in direction, additional data sources, or the elimination of some foci? Will it be acceptable to presume change, or must the changes be approved? By whom?
9. Do you know, as Kathy asked earlier, "where the review of literature fits, if the methodology used is [to be] described in a separate chapter, whether discussion of the findings is ongoing or a separate part of the report?"
10. Do your course work, outside reading, and experience enable you to bring a sense of wholeness to your proposal? What else do you need that might help you and your committee?
11. Have you examined successfully defended 'qualitative' theses for support in the areas of method and analysis?

The Defense

The proposal defense is a topic that several of the correspondents chose to recall. One correspondent, who wishes this excerpt to remain unattributed, offers the following reflections about it:

> I should mention that even though all of the committee members claimed they were open to a revised approach, at the proposal hearing two members of the committee seemed a little uncomfortable with the emergent nature of the analysis, in that they were, albeit in a speculative manner, trying to suggest general contexts for the study, such as historical comparisons. I may have to do a little bit of comparison...to satisfy three of the members who suggested it. However, I feel confident I can convince them that the objective is to bring the material in selectively, to use it where it suits my purposes, rather than doing a comprehensive comparison (which I would like to do at a later time).

Robert found "that my chosen methodologies bore the most scrutiny from my committee at the proposal defense. They appeared satisfied with the research design once I convinced them of its rigor." Kathryn recalls, "It seemed that as long as I made my decisions and assumptions explicit, there were no questions asked by my committee. This was particularly true with sample size." Pat's committee "wanted to know if I could get permission from the school district and if I would manage the technical gathering of the data."[2]

Ann credits her choice of committee members with the success of her proposal defense. Remember, too, that she had models of successful proposals to review:

> Given the feminist and qualitative awareness of my committee, no questioning occurred at the proposal defense about my use of the 1st person or my choice of conceptual framework: ideas, concepts and theories would basically emerge as I researched the question.

> In my proposal defense nothing was negotiated. My committee members (2 of whom saw my proposal only in finished form) wanted to speed me on my way and focused on making my research methodology as clear as possible and on ensuring that my question was as clear and comprehensive as possible. In the methodology area, for instance, they wanted to know exactly how I would find the individuals for my a priori categories. They suggested further questions to ask.

> My interview, by the way, is an open-ended one, with set questions or areas/themes I want to cover. I follow Ives' (1980) advice in *The Tape Recorded Interview* (pp. 62–63). The questions are in my head, and I don't get bogged down with following through mechanically, although I do know what I want to cover.

Marie reports that her proposal defense also went well:

---

[2] If you are interested in the subject of gaining entree, locate the dissertation of Vonnie B. Taylor, a participant at the 1992 Qualitative Research in Education conference at the University of Georgia (Taylor & Bonham, 1992); also see chapter 8 in Eisner's (1991) *The Enlightened Eye*.

It wasn't hard at all to get my study approved. I did what I wanted to, defended emergent designs carefully with well-placed quotes from the literature I alone was familiar with (at the time) but in which my committee was increasingly interested. When we discovered Judith Goetz, almost two years later, she was added to my committee in time for my defense; she bolstered the others' confidence in my approach.

Defense Questions: Etic/Emic

One issue that several correspondents addressed is the question of WHEN IS ENOUGH, ENOUGH? Stuart provides a descriptive response:

> During the oral examination on my dissertation proposal (i.e., before I actually began fieldwork), one of my committee members asked an extremely important question: How will you know when you are finished? When do you know that you have collected enough data and can leave the field and begin writing? I think this was an excellent question, and I frequently use it with my own students today. Quantitative researchers for the most part are able to state in advance when data collection will be completed. Based on the type of statistical analysis they want to do, they can project the sample size they need in order to generalize to the larger target population. Also, questionnaires are by their very nature fixed in time (there are just so many questions one can put into a survey). But when it comes to qualitative research, it is not always possible to know when one has collected enough data.

> The answer I gave the committee member, and the answer I work with my students on today, is the following: When I begin this study, I have a set of concerns about patient selection and placement in nursing homes, and the communicational conse-quences of particular selection and placement decisions. But this set of concerns derives from a theoretical literature (the literature on social recruitment) and does not necessarily reflect issues that are of relevance to the groups I will be studying. (In other words, I am starting with an etic question right now, and hope to understand its emic significance for the particular groups I'll be working and studying with). During the course of the ethnographic fieldwork, my initial questions will be transformed into ones that are derived from, and that are related to, the experiences of the people I am studying. Instead of coming from an abstract/general theory of social recruitment, I will be asking questions about the categories of patients that each nursing home actually, in reality, in itself recognizes and does something about in terms of finding an available bed, making a roommate decision, etc., etc. So, I am hoping that the a priori questions with which I enter the field will be transformed into community specific questions. Moreover, I wish to collect ample data to be able to leave the field when my original questions have been superceded by these community- relevant questions, and when I have collected both observational and interview data to answer these new questions.

Stuart's letter describes how original focusing questions may become irrelevant to the actual study as it progresses. Because I was also educated about the etic/emic distinction, and because I believe that qualitative research is more than a set of methods by which to get 'results', I wrote Stuart and asked if he would be willing to write a little more on the topic for those who may not be familiar with it. He agreed:

> Dear Judy,
>
> I am surprised that I was the only person to mention the etic/emic distinction; it is extremely important to me with regard to ethnographic methodology and would have thought it would be used by many of your correspondents. My dissertation advisor was/is an anthropologist, and although my degree is officially in communication, I consider myself to be an anthropologist of communication. My dissertation advisor instilled in me the importance of transforming basic observational (etic) data into categories that are culturally meaningful (emic data). Therefore, I'd have to say that the etic/emic distinction was a choice made by me but heavily influenced by my dissertation advisor.
>
> Part of the dissertation was concerned with the meaning/value/significance of being assigned to each of the different "wards" or "sections" in the two nursing homes. In other words, two wards might look identical (in terms of quality of furnishings, whether they were carpeted or covered with linoleum, type of art work on the walls) and yet function differently: one might be a prestige ward, in the sense that older/sicker/less alert patients were not placed there for residence. Emic analysis asks the question: do two comparable units (in terms of their physical/sense-related properties) function identically? do they have the same meaning/value for the members of the group? In each of the two main data chapters of the dissertation (each chapter represents an ethnographic description and social interaction analysis for one nursing home), there is therefore an analysis of the functional meaning of each of the wards/sections and a comparative analysis of the functional equivalence/non-equivalence of each of the wards visàvis the others. (For more information, see Pike, 1967.)

Summary

Knowledge of qualitative research methodologies varies across individuals; respect for persons and paradigms does as well. From my interaction with all the correspondents' materials, it seems that the amount of guidance offered, the degree of latitude to "do your own thing" and whom to please are important questions for the doctoral student to consider. Other thoughts occur: For example, where do graduate students gain the confidence to do their work? How much knowledge should a committee member assume? Is the essential purpose of the dissertation to do original work? To demonstrate research skills in an applied setting? To pass muster of the committee? Is the answer "all of the above"? Do/will/should standards of rigor vary across purposes? The following additional questions bring this chapter to a close.

QUESTIONS

12. What if your committee does not like how you propose to do your work? What is negotiable? Can you defend your choices methodologically?

13. What if, as a faculty member, you cannot condone your student's proposal? What is negotiable? Can you support your suggestions methodologically?
14. How open are you to suggestions?
15. Can you answer basic questions such as: What will be your sources of data? When is enough, enough? What types of data will be used? How much data will be used? Where and how will the data be incorporated?
16. Are you able to evaluate suggestions in terms of ethical, methodological, and contextual fit? As a student, where can you argue? Where can you compromise? Can you?

4

SUPPORTING UNDERSTANDING:
Maximizing Resources

The first three chapters of this book include many conceptions of support when using qualitative research for the doctoral dissertation. Committee members, chairs, and advisors have helped their students throughout the experience. Faculty members from other institutions have made their services available to novice researchers and faculty members less familiar with alternative methodologies. The annual Qualitative Research in Education Conference sponsored by the School of Education at the University of Georgia is a third means by which doctoral students and faculty members interested in the processes and products of qualitative research can find support. The purpose of this chapter is to address this topic more precisely. First, I provide references to the books and authors the correspondents found useful while contemplating and doing their studies. Because I include this information within the text of their letters, the appearance of the references is neither alphabetical, categorical, nor exhaustive of all books available. Additionally, because I believe it may be useful to have this information in context, and in order to save you from searching the Bibliography at the back of this volume for each individual text, I conclude this chapter with the full citations of each of the books the correspondents mention. The Bibliography at the end of the book, therefore, contains only the material that is either directly cited elsewhere or which directly influenced the writing of this book.

Second, and in addition to the perspectives already described, I discuss other people as resources. Formal study groups as well as less formal relationships including friends, family, and other faculty members also support the doctoral research process. Finally, I choose to highlight the concept of time and the issue of money as supporting (or thwarting!) doctoral studies.

Books

Ann mentions several books that helped her prepare for the proposal defense:

> At the beginning, but not during the writing, I found books such as Yin's (1982) helpful. It was too prescriptive later when I was well away into creating my proposal.

38

After I finished my proposal and before the defense I found Marshall and Rossman (1989), Patton (1990), Bogdan and Biklen (1982), Sternberg (1981), and Ives (1980) helpful in tightening certain sections (methodology and analysis) and preparing for the defense of the proposal.

A book I admire for its readability and entertainment value in what both the researchers say and the interviewed say (long quotes) is Aisenberg and Harrington's (1988) *Women of Academe: Outsiders in the Sacred Grove.*

Another text mentioned by many correspondents is Glaser and Strauss' (1967) volume, *The Discovery of Grounded Theory.* Additionally, my anonymous correspondent did some thinking about examples of qualitative research and writes:

The most qualitative case study I know of in social science is Carlos Castandeda's research on Don Juan, resulting in his controversial dissertation. My dissertation is not nearly as qualitative and subjective. On the other hand, it is far from quantitative.... I do refer to the case study method which I used as inspired by Mitchell (1983).

Kathryn writes that she "found LeCompte (1982) useful to anticipate issues from quantitatively trained researchers and tried to make explicit a number of decisions about the research."

Gretchen remembers that she:

...included the table from Guba and Lincoln (1981, p. 104) in my discussion of rigor and validity; I also quoted from page 113 where they discuss threats to validity. The issue of reliability was of most concern to the part of the study dealing with coding decisions, and I dealt with that using Holsti's composite reliability formula (1968, p.137). My committee was satisfied; some journal reviewers have been critical of this formula.

Nancy writes that she:

... swallowed the assumptions underlying the naturalistic paradigm hook, line, and sinker. I also looked to Lincoln and Guba (1985) regarding trustworthiness criteria, attempting, as they suggest, to triangulate data from different sources (interviews, observations, archival records, student transcripts, etc.). *Naturalistic Inquiry* was my dissertation project bible.

Jean also refers to Lincoln and Guba (1985):

I used Lincoln and Guba's text, *Naturalistic Inquiry,* when taking my first qualitative research class and turned to it throughout my work on my dissertation. The clearly defined processes were invaluable. I wish more people who conduct qualitative research would use the protocols they suggest. I am aghast at the number of professors and teachers conducting research in the Chicago area who do not get permission from parents and children before using their work or are even aware that that should be a consideration. When I mention anonymity and confidentiality, they act as though these are words whose meanings are foreign to them. I can't help but wonder WHO taught them to do qualitative research....Mishler (1986), Carini (1979) and Duckworth (1987) were each tremendously helpful.

Marie, who successfully defended her thesis in 1982, writes that "the most helpful single book I read was Schatzman and Strauss (1973)." Pat, who defended her thesis 8 years later, also found the Schatzman and Strauss book useful. Additionally, Robert suggested that Spradley (1980) and Taylor and Bogdan (1984) are useful texts for qualitative researchers.

Since I began the research for this volume, many other books about qualitative research have been published. A quick browse in the library and in the bibliographies of the aforementioned books is one way to increase your material resource base. Getting hold of publishers' flyers for new books is another. Course work and bibliographies of completed dissertations provide additional resources as well.

Authors

Carol was fortunate enough to have a 'dual' resource base, a book and its author! She writes:

> My committee included Sherman Stanage, PhD, who is solidly in the camp of doing qualitative research. His book (1987) helped, as did discussions with him and the rest of my committee.

Nancy Zeller (working with Egon Guba) and Marie Nelson (working with Judith Goetz) each had a resource base that went beyond a text. Several other correspondents, including Jean Stevenson and Pat Garlikov, had similar interactions with individuals highly regarded in the field of qualitative research. Experts are a valuable resource to novice qualitative researchers.

QUESTIONS

1. What books are available to you? Have you searched in disciplines other than your own? Might faculty members in other departments be able to help you locate resources? Might your peers? Course work?
2. Are there any qualitative research experts in your department? On campus? At nearby universities?
3. Is the environment in your department, school/college, and graduate school supportive of qualitative research? Is this important to know before you begin?

Other People

Perhaps nothing has been less clearly written about but remains most crucial to the experience of doing qualitative research than the aspect of relationships. Student–

committee interactions were discussed in chapter 2, but there are additional relationships forged, maintained, or broken during the dissertation process. I will begin this section with the formal relationships particularly established to support the process and end up with those that are more personal.

Jean remembers one person whose attitudes and influence can directly promote an environment conducive to qualitative research. She writes, "The Dean when I began my studies was very inclusive in his acceptance of all forms of research. The current Dean continues to support that philosophical bent."

Study Groups.   Study groups are another positive influence supporting the doing of qualitative research. Maria, who completed her dissertation at the University of Pittsburgh in 1982, wrote at length about the value of the one in which she participated. Much of her reflection is included here:

RECOLLECTIONS AND REFLECTIONS ON THE DISSERTATION
The Dissertation Study Group
Maria Piantanida, PhD
July 3, 1990

My advisor had not been satisfied with the quality of her own dissertation and had been considering ways in which she might help her own advisees do more credible studies. She also believes that the dissertation should not be a meaningless academic exercise, but a substantive first step in establishing a student's professional/research agenda and helping him/her to become part of a scholarly community. Her own thinking about the links between theory and practice had been evolving, and she had been finding ways to theorize from practice-based data. The piece that was missing for her was the epistemological framework for defending 'non-traditional' dissertations. By the later 1970s, she was ready to figure out the missing piece. At the same time, four of her doctoral students had reached the proposal stage, and she suggested the idea of forming a Dissertation Study Group. We all agreed (taking it on faith that this would be a good idea and help us with the dissertation). She made it very clear that she did not have answers, and that we would be seeking answers together. Although all of us view her as our teacher and mentor, we also see her as a fellow learner and explorer. The collegiality that evolved among all of us was one of the most gratifying outcomes of the Study Group.

Our advisor knew that it would not be particularly easy to convince other faculty in the School of Education about the legitimacy of our dissertations. She began to lay some groundwork. I'm vague about the dates at this point, but somewhere around this time (1980?), she catalyzed a one-day conference on grounded theory. She invited Phyllis Stern to come to Pittsburgh and give a presentation to students and faculty. She was supported in this effort by a colleague of hers who had guided some dissertations using grounded theory. That conference sort of 'launched' our efforts.

I was the first member of the Study Group to begin working on my proposal and to take it to committee. My three peers were also working on theirs at the same time. We were so close together in the process I tend to think of us as going through it simultaneously. We learned from each other, from our experience/encounters with committee members, from the references we were finding, and from the ways in which we struggled with the epistemological underpinnings of our research.

I'm not sure when, but gradually other students joined the Study Group. Six of us met together on a regular basis and finished interpretive dissertations. Another woman came periodically to our meetings. My advisor was a member of her committee but was not her advisor. Of all of us, this woman got caught between the two research paradigms, and her advisor would not approve her writing her study in an interpretive way. (Interestingly enough, she, too, used a case study method.)

Two other women began to meet with the Group about the time the first six of us were finished. They worked more independently than the rest of us did, but we still consider them part of the group. Another woman had finished her dissertation before the Study Group was formed. Her own intellectual rigor led her to conceptualize two dissertations—the first quantitative, which left her with the feeling of 'so what'; a second version that was more qualitative which addressed this issue. Although she did not participate in the Group, she joined us later when my advisor was creating opportunities for us to present our work at conferences. We view her as a group member, because the spirit of her inquiry and her commitment to rigorous inquiry makes her a kindred spirit. My advisor's colleague from ASU is also considered a Study Group member, because he served on many of our committees as a mentor and guide. So, when I refer to the Dissertation Study Group, I mean all 12 of us....I've gone into such depth about this, because it represents a significant aspect of my own dissertation experience (and I think the experience of the others). We were not alone; we were not fighting epistemological battles by ourselves; we became, in a sense, our own community of scholars; we were a critical mass that could not be ignored or discounted as 'flakes' who just wanted to do 'quick and dirty' qualitative studies....

When we started the Study Group, we tended to use 'grounded theory' as the umbrella term to describe the nature of the research we were undertaking. As members of the group began to conceptualize and design their studies, they began to use other methods (e.g., case study, retrospective case study, hermeneutic study). We used 'naturalistic' for a while, and then conceptual (because AERA had proposed that term). Currently, we use the term 'interpretive' research to distinguish what we did from more positivist studies....

As we gained experience, we began to see that each study had a structure unique to its purpose, process and results. The final dissertation documents did not follow the routine formula. They had an integrity of structure that emerged from the process and best communicated the results of the inquiry. In my own case, I wanted to submit my dissertation for publication as a book that would be read by practitioners who would have little understanding of or patience for reading a research rationale. Therefore, I put my discussion of research methods in Chapter 4. Chapter 3 contained the substantive theory of practice that I had generated from my study. Chapter 5 contained a formal theory of professional practice that I generated as a result of my reflections on the research process and myself as an evolving scholar. One of my committee members argued during my defense that a dissertation is a dissertation, not a book. We went back and forth about this, but in the end, we agreed to disagree and the format remained unchanged.

One of the consistent pieces of feedback we have received from faculty is that the documents are extremely readable and that the writing has a vitality to it. I believe that these qualities resulted, at least in part, from the fact that we could not follow a cut and dried formula and do justice to the knowledge generated through our research and the richness of our data.

Maria's rich description offers an abundance of material for doctoral students and committee members to explore. Maria also provided some materials generated by the Study Group:

The following comments on the study group experience come from the members of the study group. After the comments were collected, they were clustered under major headings that indicate the general categories of benefit of the study group. It is interesting to note that in almost all cases, we ended up with comments in each category suggesting our shared perceptions of the value of the Study Group experience.

EXPLORING RESEARCH ISSUES

The study group is where I:

- learn more about research, discuss my own research and learn how to direct others in the research process.
- gain familiarity with research terms.
- have an opportunity to formulate the rationale for my conceptual research in a supportive, yet critical group.
- have an opportunity to understand the nuances of the research paradigm.

The study group provided:

- an arena for collecting and exchanging important articles relating to conceptual research.
- an ongoing opportunity to get feedback on each phase of the research as it progressed.
- a double-edged research situation, since members were not only conducting their independent studies, but were also studying the nature of conceptual research.
- a forum within which to develop a lexicon for conceptual research. (We have charged ourselves, however, to remain vigilant against the dangers of exclusionary language.)
- a forum for my ideas.

PROVIDING PERSONAL SUPPORT

In the study group, I found:

- the sharing of concerns—in both the intellectual pursuits and the emotional realm.
- affirmation of the scholarly part of me by people who shared rather than disparaged my values about research and the dissertation process.

- a mechanism for seeing myself in the process; for sorting out my own idiosyncrasies from the nature of the process. To get re-energized rather than wallow in my blocks.
- support and reassurance about what is 'normal' in the dissertation process.
- a sympathetic support group for members suffering through research anxieties.
- an enjoyable social setting that combined stimulating conversation with good food and drink.

ENCOURAGING SCHOLARLY DEVELOPMENT

As a result of participating in the study group, I was able to:

- identify relevant theoretical literature and process what it meant.
- refine ideas; hone concepts.
- exchange materials on content and methodology.
- have a place to make a contribution, to use what I was learning to help others learn; a place to have a sense of satisfaction and accomplishment.
- The study group for me represents 'the university' in the finest sense of the word, that is, a community of scholars engaged in mutual learning and discovery.
- The study group has helped alleviate dissertation post-partum by providing a forum for continued scholarship, publication and professional application of dissertation learning.
- The study group satisfies my need to share the insights and experiences of the research and conceptualization process.
- The study group has provided feedback and questions to help me refine and clarify ideas.
- The study group satisfies a basic need I have as an educator to pass learning on, to perpetuate a cycle of learning.
- The study group has evolved from a social/support oriented group for me to one that is goal and task oriented. This new orientation makes it possible for the study group to make new kinds of contributions to conceptual research and to reach a larger audience than ourselves.

Yet another product of the Study Group is a set of questions they generated around the issue of quality in qualitative research. Because I find them thought-provoking, I include them here:

CRITERIA FOR JUDGING QUALITY RESEARCH

Verite: Does the work ring true? Is it consistent with accepted knowledge in the field? Or if it departs, does it address why? Does it fit within the context of the literature? Is it intellectually honest and authentic?

Integrity (as in architecture):   Is the work structurally sound? Does it hang together? In a piece of research, is the design or research rationale logical, appropriate, and identifiable within a paradigm?

Rigor: Is there sufficient depth of intellect, rather than superficial or simplistic reasoning?

Utility: Usefulness, professionally relevant. Does it make a contribution to the field? Does the piece have a clearly recognizable professional audience?

Vitality: Is it important, meaningful, nontrivial? Does it have a sense of vibrancy, intensity, excitement of discovery? Is the proper personae (or voice) used for the researcher or author? Do metaphors, images, or visuals communicate powerfully?

Aesthetics: Is it enriching, pleasing to anticipate and experience? Does it give me insight into some universal part of my educational self? Does it touch my spirit in some way?

Although questions can be thought-provoking, they can also be an overwhelming burden. What I find of value among all the previous comments and questions is the fact that they were generated by a group of individuals working together to figure out how to undertake and complete qualitative dissertations. In the case of Maria's Study Group, more than two heads were better than one.

Others among the correspondents also found value in study groups. Jean recalls:

> Some of the faculty and graduate students met once a week for the Naturalistic Inquiry Seminar. It was a non-credit seminar which served as a forum for sharing books, research, and ideas. I MISS IT. There was also an informal group of faculty and (usually doctoral) graduate students who met as a writing support group. I MISS THAT GROUP, TOO. We graduate students would meet formally at least once a month for lunch to talk, share current research, and fret. We also met for lunch, coffee, etc. much more frequently. We were a relatively 'tight' group; membership changed as students graduated and moved on or began their research. The faculty encouraged our meeting together. It was through this group that I got the name of my typist.

Tim also recommends forming a study group.

> You are not alone. Seek out the advice and sympathetic ears of your colleagues. We have an organized group of graduate students who share problems, ideas and bland cafeteria food. I have thought that it might be a good idea to get to know some of the qualitative-oriented students in other fields here at the university in order to share concerns about qualitative research. (Being qualitatively oriented, we would seek out better food.) I have met a lot of students at the University of Georgia's January conferences on qualitative research, so I do not feel I am alone as far as qualitative research goes.

One aspect of support for doing qualitative research is knowing that you are not the only one who has questions and concerns.

QUESTIONS

4. What are the possibilities of forming a study group? Is there already one around inquiry issues in your—or another— department? Might you enjoy a study group? Do you know of any faculty members who might be interested?

Respondents.   Another perspective on personal support comes from two correspondents who explicitly mentioned that their research respondents were supportive of their efforts. Paula, who studied the power communication skills of female college presidents, recalls:

> Judith, you specifically asked me about the reaction and support from the participants. Some of their comments are in the methodology section which is enclosed. I kept their comments in a notebook and took notes as I spoke with each during the initial telephone interview. The support from each with whom I spoke was great (whether they were able to participate or not)! One called the study provocative. Some encouraged me to develop a training program after I completed. Nearly all were friendly, easy to talk to and had ideas and comments of their own regarding the study. One told me that people were rarely interested in what she did; she thought that most women in her position would find it a 'rare pleasure' to have me spend a week with them. I have more of these types of comments if you need them.

Jean also speaks highly of her two research participants:

> The two writers I selected were incredible! Not only had they donated their papers— an exposure of self that can't be imagined—but they were also willing to answer all sorts of questions from me....I sent written questions to each of them and also had an opportunity to interview both of them. The questions I asked were idiosyncratic. I did not have a list I asked both writers.

Family, Friends, New Colleagues.   Although family can also be an important support relationship, Jean is the only correspondent who wrote about it. As you may recall, comments about her family lace her letters with an important, intimate connection (e.g., chapter 1, p. 10). I am curious about this notion of a support system; while I was a doctoral student, I heard stories about how some relationships break up because of the intensity and single-mindedness of the dissertation experience. I can remember how little time I seemed to have for anything or anyone else. Who supports the families of focused qualitative researchers? For how long must families be supportive? In the following excerpt, correspondent Jane Patton places questions like these in context. She also kept me updated as her research progressed from June 1990 through the end of April 1991, when she defended; her writing has an explicit, present tense quality to it:

> A classmate, who was my roommate during our residency, had her defense this week. Of course her study was quantitative!! I feel a bit of jealousy but also reassured that one actually can finish! I know I have to push myself hard at this point to keep up the momentum. Whew!
>
> I have noticed that I have slacked off on working on my dissertation, mostly because I am now teaching, and the job has kept me running. But now I feel I have to say 'no' to everything else (as much as possible) and make the dissertation first priority.

We all have work lives and home lives. During the dissertation experience, the challenge seems to be in finding the time to do anything (or everything!) well. Several correspondents, including Jane, share the benefits of talking with their friends as they work through their first qualitative research experience. Jane continues:

8/17/90

Dear Judy,

I've gotten into data analysis, and some pieces of the puzzle are beginning to fall into place. I have found it very helpful to talk to Cindy periodically; she is also doing a qualitative study. We are attending different universities, are in different degree programs (hers is a PhD in nursing; mine an EdD) and we have different designs (hers is ethnographic and only uses interviews; mine is a case study and uses several forms of data). However, when we get together, we reassure one another, clarify and give fresh perspectives. Also, we aren't as judgmental as a professor might be, so we can say anything! That support has been really valuable for both of us.

I've noticed some emotional swings in doing this project. Cindy has too. I don't know how much is just part of doing a dissertation and how much is amplified by doing a qualitative study. We both have said how 'stupid' we feel when we get frustrated. Sometimes I think, "This is so easy; I'm really on a roll." Other times I think I have nothing and it's all garbage. Cindy also reports similar feelings.

10/19/90

.... When I told my advisor about the new friend I've made (Cindy), she agreed that having someone to talk to WHO UNDERSTANDS QUALITATIVE RESEARCH is really valuable. Cindy and I have continued to benefit from brainstorming together and reassuring each other.

In the following excerpt, Jean describes a friendship that offers additional strengths and support:

A friend (who is now a faculty member at another university) and I took my first and her only qualitative research methods course together. She is an incredible statistician. If I want to do anything with statistics, I'll turn to her. She understands qualitative research and why it is done. She chooses not to do it, because she does not feel she writes well enough. If a student comes to her with a problem that involves qualitative research, she will guide the student to someone who conducts qualitative research and writes well. She will do this not because she isn't capable but because this is not where her passion or expertise lies. She and I have had many discussions surrounding this issue and have decided that a qualitative researcher must be a writer. She doesn't feel that writing is as important in quantitative studies....A well-written statistical paper is a gift and great, but the use or abuse of the statistical data is what matters. I know that she and I respect each other as teachers, researchers and scholars. We have both come away from the class and our discussions with a healthy respect for the amount of work involved in conducting any research.

QUESTIONS

5. Do your friends and family know the level of mental and emotional energy 'handling ambiguity' requires? Do you know by now that you CAN do this, with confidence, support, and grace? Do you know you are not alone?

Time and Money

There are still other struggles and tradeoffs facing novice qualitative researchers that have not been clearly or fully articulated, even here. The need for and pressures of time and money are described in a variety of ways. For example, Gretchen offers an example of the kind of juggling act that can occur:

> I did my graduate work, one course at a time, while teaching high school French and Spanish full time. I used a sabbatical from high school to complete my on-campus residency requirement. As a 46-year-old student beginning PhD work in a new field, I had planned to take the full seven years but finished in five. There was a constant time crunch. Given a variety of other events beyond my control, my committee advanced the dates for several key milestones. My preliminary exam was moved ahead because my advisor was sure I was ready (even though I wanted several months more to review). I passed all parts the first time, so I can't complain, but it was very stressful to do it that way. Then, I was going to spend the summer of 1985 analyzing my pilot study and preparing to defend the proposal; when I came back June 8 from taking 45 high school Spanish students to Mexico, I found out that one of my committee members was moving away in two weeks! The committee told me to crank out the 75-page proposal immediately, and they approved it June 18. A year later, they put pressure on me to finish everything by late October in order to meet deadlines for November graduation. I think this was because they wanted to nominate my dissertation for a national award and the following year there would be two others from the department that looked as if they had award-winning potential. (My dissertation was among the top eight nationally for the 1986 Redding Award, but didn't make the final cut.)

One correspondent describes another resource that was simultaneously a constraint on the dissertation effort:

> My dissertation was odd, because I used the facilities of another institution to complete it....I would travel down to the city, stay with friends for two to three days, and work there....Originally, I had asked the curator of the collection (a PhD, who, by the way and along with her staff, was wonderful to me) to serve on my committee, but the then Dean of the Graduate School began throwing up roadblocks. I was given the distinct impression that a dissertation done at 'our' university should have only 'our' university faculty on its committee.

Several other correspondents mentioned that along the way to completing their research, either their major advisor or an important committee member died. The human connection, even to issues of time and money, is always there. Jean writes:

> I did receive a year long scholarship that made life easier. Otherwise, my husband and I financed my work. I was an instructor for three semesters and supervised student teachers, which helped.

In a postscript to her original letter, Paula adds:

> I forgot to mention the size of my dissertation—215 pages...much too large and too expensive to have typed and duplicated. It cost over $750 for typing, editing, and duplicating—and I had very few mistakes (or it would have cost much more!) Will you address this issue?

Paula's dissertation is actually quite small compared to some (Stuart's = 500 pages, Jean's = 415 pages, Jane's = 390) and comparable to others (Nancy's = 230 pages, or mine = 282). The cost of production is worth investigating and considering when planning to undertake qualitative research for the dissertation. As another correspondent relates, there are other costs as well:

> I was also helped through the maze of institutional barbed wire by my typist. A longtime, respected graduate school typist, she was able to 'catch' and question things which were almost clear. She was also a 'walking style manual'. However, the outside reader was poor. She editorialized and questioned the inclusion of items suggested by my committee. Her constant markings in what I presumed to be the final text required a total re-run of my dissertation and an additional $50.00.

QUESTIONS

6. What is your time schedule? Is it flexible? What is your 'life load' like (i.e., what other responsibilities also demand your time? Your mental and emotional energy?) Whose schedule are you on? Qualitative studies take longer than quantitative ones...can you 'cut yourself some slack' once in awhile and not feel guilty? Do you remember the word...FUN ???

7. Are any of the faculty members with whom you are working planning sabbaticals in the near future? Retirement? Professional moves? Is your timetable compatible? Can it be adjusted? What are the tradeoffs? Are they worth it?

8. What are the costs of this effort in strictly financial terms? Are there departmental scholarships available for the dissertation year? Is there travel support if you choose to give a presentation about your work, or are you working full-time? What is realistic for you? What can you afford?

9. How much are you really on your own? How willing are you to enlist the support of others? Can you 'be nice' to yourself and still feel you are making progress?

10. Can you type?

Summary

Much more could be written about the nature and value of dissertation support systems. Support may come from external resources or internal goals, from the university or a child. The stories of Marie and Stuart offered here enable us to view contemporary possibilities and constraints from a different perspective:

November 9, 1990

Dear Judy,

I've been wondering where I put your letters for weeks, but today, having set aside a whole day for housecleaning, I found them. Given the constant state of pressure and denial (smile) I experience, let me respond now before I lose them again.... Advance copies of my new book, *At the Point of Need: Teaching Basic and ESL Writers*, which is hot off the press, arrived today from Boynton/Cook. (It's a perfect example of the negotiations—or more precisely, the sacrifices—faculty as well as graduate students have to make to do the kind of research we do.) Since I'm between deadlines right now, let me begin.

My case may be different from those of some people you study, for I had very few negotiations to make during the process of my dissertation. That does not mean I always did what I wanted to, however. When I was first in my doctoral program, quantitative research was all that I was taught, and in 1970 I left Georgia A.B.D. (all but dissertation) because I could not find a dissertation topic I was willing to devote a year of my life to doing. At that point I had taken at least 20 quarter hours in research design and statistics, courses I found to be extremely interesting and intellectually stimulating. It was the topics of studies that could be done using those methods that were neither interesting nor stimulating to me.

When I returned eight years later, I had to revalidate my course work, retake my comprehensive exam, and retake the final course in the research sequence which was still entirely quantitative. In my department, however, interest in case study research had been aroused by the work of Janet Emig and Don Graves, but I did not want to do case studies. I wanted to study the classrooms of writers who teach writing; I had no idea how I would go about selecting them, for I had known many writers who taught quite traditionally, disregarding entirely what they told me about how they themselves wrote.

Although Judith Goetz (who with Marki LeCompte was working on an important book on qualitative research in education) was already at my institution, my male mentors did not know her then and did not know she was teaching a course in qualitative methods in the Social Science Education department. I was entirely on my own when it came to preparing myself methodologically. I read and read and read, dozens of articles and books, until, finally, after about three months of following blind alleys—I had never heard the term ethnography—I discovered Schatzman and Strauss (1973) and a number of anthropological methodologists. The night I found Schatzman and Strauss I stayed up all night reading. In symbolic interactionism I knew I had found what I needed for my study.

Stuart, who while on sabbatical leave in Australia was responding to a question I had about his Table of Contents (see Appendix C), also enables us to appreciate the changing times:

> You asked about the NOTES section at the end of each chapter: I don't have a copy of the dissertation here with me, so I cannot refer to the particular notes you are speaking of. Overall, I decided to create a notes section at the end of each chapter, rather than footnotes, because when I wrote the dissertation I used a typewriter and not a personal computer or word processor. As you can imagine, when I had to submit revised versions of chapters after they had been read and critiqued by my dissertation advisor, it was much easier doing a cut-and-paste job on pages of text without worrying about footnotes on the bottom. It seems hard to imagine today, but only ten years ago people like me were working without benefit of personal computers, without any software that with a simple command can renumber footnotes, etc., etc. So, there was no requirement which dictated the use of endnotes; I just found it a much easier way of handling note material.

Although I was a grouch at the time I had to learn how to use the computer and word processing software in order to get the dissertation completed, after reading Stuart's account I have begun to treat my computer with slightly more regard. Support doesn't have to be human. Even chocolate works!

References

Aisenberg, N., & Harrington, M. (1988). *Women of academe: Outsiders in the sacred grove*. Amherst: University of Massachusetts Press.

Bogdan, R., & Biklen, S. (1982). *Qualitative research for education: An introduction to theory and methods*. Needham Heights, MA: Allyn & Bacon.

Carini, P. F. (1979). *The art of seeing and the visibility of the person*. Grand Forks, ND: North Dakota Study Group on Evaluation.

Duckworth, E. (1987). *'The having of wonderful Ideas' and other essays on teaching and learning*. New York: Teachers College Press

Glaser, B. G., & Strauss, L. (1967). *The discovery of grounded theory*. New York: Aldine de Gruyter.

Guba, E. G., & Lincoln, Y. S. (1981). *Effective evaluation*. San Francisco: Jossey-Bass.

Holstoi, O. R. (1968). *Content analysis for the social sciences*. Reading, MA: Addison-Wesley.

Ives, E. D. (1980). *The tape-recorded interview: A manual for field workers in folklore and oral history*. Knoxville: University of Tennessee Press.

LeCompte, M. D., & Goetz, J. P. (1982). Problems of reliability in ethnographic research. *Review of Educational Research, 52*, 31–60.

Lincoln, Y. S., & Guba, E. G. (1985). *Naturalistic inquiry*. Beverly Hills: Sage.

Marshall, C., & Rossman, G. (1989). *Designing qualitative research*. Beverly Hills: Sage.

Mishler, E. G. (1986). *Research interviewing: Context and narrative*. Cambridge, MA: Harvard University Press.

Mitchell, C. J. (1983). Case and situational analysis. *Sociological Review, 31*(2), 187–211.

Patton, M. Q. (1990). *Qualitative evaluation and research methods*. Beverly Hills: Sage.

Schatzman, L. & Strauss, A. (1973). *Field research: Strategies for a natural sociology*. Englewood Cliffs, NJ: Prentice-Hall.

Spradley, J. P. (1980). *Participant observation*. NY: Holt, Rinehart & Winston.

Stanage, S. (1987). *Adult education and phenomenological research: New directions for theory, practice and research.* Malabar, FL: R.E. Krieger.

Sternberg, D. (1981). *How to complete and survive a doctoral dissertation.* New York: St. Martin's Press.

Taylor, S. J., & Bogdan, R. (1984). *Introduction to qualitative research methods.* New York: Wiley.

Yin, R. K. (1984). *Case study research: Design and methods.* Newbury Park, CA: Sage.

5

UNDERSTANDING BY FOCUSING:
Connecting Focus, Literature, and Ownership

Focus and Literature

Research texts often assume that the researcher has a problem to pursue. Little time is spent discussing what is and is not a problem; more time is spent suggesting where to look for one. Determining a focus in qualitative research usually includes examining and reexamining the research context, changing one's mind, and giving up preconceived notions of what is important. As suggested in chapter 1, understanding the focus occurs nearer to the middle and the end—as opposed to the beginning—of the inquiry. Finding focus is intimately linked to who an individual is as well as to how he or she thinks and what there is to think about. A focus may 'emerge' from context, but it actually takes shape as a result of how an individual looks at a given context, what is perceived, and what that individual determines to do with all of that "stuff." If a statistical analogy might be used, finding focus is, in a sense, the result of an 'interaction effect' of person and context. Two questions that many novice researchers have remain unexplored: Where does the original combination of thoughts come from? Which thoughts do I choose? Several correspondents share their reflections about how they found a focus and what that focus/interest means to them. Nancy writes:

> I knew I was interested in meta-inquiry and that I didn't want to do and report on an experimental project. I further knew that I wanted to write a dissertation that developed and provided convincing support for an <u>argument</u> rather than one which collected and tinkered with data until I found an argument the data would support. That statement contains a redundancy, but so few dissertations nowadays develop and support an argument that maybe it's worth repeating. I would guess that my background in speech (B.S.) and English (M.A.) had a lot to do with how my dissertation project was conceived and carried out.

Kathy recalls:

> Focus was a problem at the onset, that is, keeping focused on the questions that guide the study. Michael Patton helped at last year's Qualitative Research in Education

Conference (School of Education, UGA, 1990) when he told me that it is all right to talk about the big picture and that it is not necessary to look carefully at all of the happenings that pose interesting questions.

Kathryn explicitly links her thinking to the literature in her field; she notes how her understandings grew and changed:

I started my doctoral education interested in the physiologic stress response and how to reduce stress for acute myocardial infarction (AMI) patients in the coronary care setting. Before I began course work in a new content area (stress and coping) I really believed that the problem was well understood, and that it was simply a matter of going about creating the right set of experiments to find the 'best' ways to reduce stress for this group of patients. However, as I explored the general and specific stress literature and tried to apply it to clinical experiences, I began to recognize the limits of current understanding. Pieces were missing; what was described by authorities simply did not make sense...I still quite clearly recall the quarter when I decided that too little was known about what was happening, or at least it was not documented, to begin to develop experiments. In other words, it was a qualitative not a quantitative problem. This was, I am sure you will understand, a very exciting and awesome process...changing world views and trying to integrate alternative research paradigms with those of an entire education in the sciences. I was, after all, a critical care nurse accustomed to measuring and quantifying. It was just that I was also coming to recognize that the problem I wanted answers to, i.e., the best way to reduce stress for AMI patients, was more complex than addressed in relevant literature; there was much unknown that I was just beginning to acknowledge. I now very honestly believe that we have delayed our development as a science because we have tried to approach all nursing/patient questions from the quantitative approach. We can change that, however. In a way this paralleled my frustration with the fact that, despite all my prior education, I had not as yet encountered a way to handle things, such as observations and hunches.

I think there is more to why my dissertation has its form. For a qualitative study I have a lengthy review of the literature. The purpose was to describe why this study needed to be done, although there had already been a fair amount of research on the subject. I wanted to find the holes. The review also served to introduce support for the use of a theory to direct inquiry in a direction not used before with this group; my interview guide was developed from coping theory. I wanted my committee to know what I knew about what had already been done, why I thought it did not adequately address the situation and why I was going to go about the study in the way I was about to describe. These were my decision rules for what I included. I am sure I read about it somewhere. Let me share the conclusions to the literature review chapter to flesh that out:

"Interest by clinicians and researchers in how acute myocardial infarction (AMI) patients cope early in illness has focused primarily on the use and benefits of denial. While a few investigators have suggested that AMI patients use additional means of coping that may be as important to recovery as denial, the denial paradigm continues to dominate current thought on the subject. Little data have been accumulated regarding use of various coping strategies by AMI patients: however, the rich descriptions of coping gathered from patients dealing with other illnesses suggests that this limited view may be the result of conceptualization of coping and assessment methods rather than lack of varied coping efforts by AMI patients. Though research in this area is limited, studies suggest that supporting or failing to support various coping efforts can have a significant impact on recovery. The theory of coping proposed by Lazarus offers a useful framework directing further inquiry into how AMI patients cope." (p. 28)

Like Kathryn, Ann also combines the review of the literature with the focus and significance of her study:

For the literature review in the proposal, 10 pages only seemed to be what everyone else had done and what my advisor wanted. I wanted my lit review to do more than set the stage for my study; I wanted it to be useful, definitive, up-to-date and to be an entire chapter of my dissertation. My advisor didn't complain about this. I got the impression that if I wanted to do this amount of work, didn't get bogged down in it, and it didn't hold up the process of completion, then it was fine to go ahead.

One correspondent comments about the ongoing nature of the literature review as it relates to changing research foci and a familiar question:

A third decision, based on my major professor's preference, was that I continuously review the literature throughout the study. Although I found doing this to be a lot of work, it was helpful. When one reads the literature and then notes what appears to be important, there is a good chance something is left out. In collecting the data and interpreting and analyzing it, I found that there was literature supporting some of my findings—literature which I had failed to include in the first drafts of the literature review.

The question of "how much literature review is enough?" or "when should I quit reviewing the literature?" was always on my mind. Even during the 2 weeks preceding my defense date, I wanted to review the literature on a particular topic because my third reader said I had ignored the literature in this area, even though the discussion of it appeared only in the final analysis. Also at the defense, I was told that I had 'ignored' certain literature, yet I had read over 100 references for the review. When is enough, enough???

Other correspondents mention additional concerns regarding the focus and the appropriate literature. Pat writes, "The review was located throughout the dissertation. I only found the most appropriate literature descriptor, children's discourse, after [emphasis added] the completion of the dissertation." Another correspondent recalls:

The literature review included two sections. Although I chose to cite one of the most widely quoted scholars in our field, I found myself educating my committee members about this work. I doubt if my advisor even read the second section of the literature review; none of the committee members had any questions or comments about that section.

QUESTIONS

1. What are the current influences on your thinking—educational background, personal experiences, contemporary course work, faculty interests? How will you choose a focus? Can you identify areas of interest to you, ideas that might be fun to explore? What are you curious about?
2. Do you have any idea how you will sort out 'important' questions from unimportant ones? 'Big' ones from 'little' ones? How will you keep track of your ideas?
3. Are there particular areas of focus compatible for study with qualitative research methodology? Does your knowledge of qualitative research help sort categories of potential topics? How? Should it?
4. What is the difference, if any, between method and methodology? Is this an important question to consider when focusing a research effort? Why or why not?
5. How long does the review of the literature have to be for (a) the prospectus and (b) the dissertation?
6. Where does the review of the literature belong? In one chapter? Throughout the dissertation? Who says?
7. Which literatures are important to review? Appropriate to review? When should they be reviewed? When is enough, enough? Who says?

Finding focus, staying focused, and gaining a final sense of direction is a personal, human issue in that it is not merely a matter of identifying an external question to answer. Focusing can be simultaneously more uncomfortable and more enlightening than just finding a question. Nancy's reflections and the following disclosure of another correspondent provide a more explicit and intimate sense of the extremely personal focus required when one is the human research instrument:

> One thing I discovered about conducting case studies is that you can never anticipate the ways in which things can go wrong and that you'd better be prepared to undergo some kind of change as a result of doing the case study. I believe that a personal transformation in understanding that moves from logic/reason toward intuition/emotion is inevitable and, further, that the case researcher must be willing to see her/himself as a wrong thing in a right world in order to be transformed into the filter through which experience is shaped and given meaning. This transformation, which cannot be foreseen or planned for, may involve learning to view things in a simpler way than academics—even naturalists—are used to.

Another correspondent shares the following:

> ...regarding the methodology, there is a section on me as the researcher. I found this difficult to write because I am a very private person and because of my personal

history. When having to compose that section, I felt 'naked.' Am I making sense? You see, I am talking about the incident as an eight year old, when I was told that I had to control my temper. I learned to control my temper, but in controlling my temper, I also learned to control all my emotions, which is both good and not so good.... Was my research biased? Probably, but not more than other research, whether statistical or qualitative. I believe that all research is biased, because each researcher brings his or her experiences, expectations, and judgments to the 'laboratory' or 'field'.

Ownership

Although finding focus is a personal endeavor, there was little discussion of bias from any of the correspondents, except as a consideration of method. However, the concept of ownership of the thesis was brought up again and again. One of the 'feelings' about what it means to do qualitative research appears to be a strong, definite sense of direct, personal connection with the processes and product, in large part, I think, because of the connection between thinking and writing. Jean is just one of the correspondents whose letters suggested this topic:

Earlier in this letter, I mentioned choice and ownership and the roles both play in my own work...but I believe that being allowed to make choices concerning topic, etc. has a profound effect on ownership and ultimately on the development of a strong sense of responsibility for the piece. In *Lessons from a Child: On the Teaching and Learning of Writing*, Lucy McCormick Calkins (1983) says, "When children are makers of reading, they gain a sense of ownership over their reading. As we've seen again and again, owners are different from tenants" (p.156). Choice is the key. In writing process classrooms, the writers choose their own topics. No one tells them what to write. The power of choice gives the writer involved ownership and is "awesome" to behold; with that ownership comes responsibility.

Jean continues, mentioning ownership again as connected to the focus of her study, "I threw objectivity out the window in the sense that one of the criteria used in selecting the authors for the study was that I liked their work and would use it. Kathy Gershman gave me a very good bit of advice about selecting subjects—'You MUST be willing to live with them for the rest of your life.'" My anonymous correspondent reflects on ownership less explicitly and writes, "I assumed the dissertation would be worthwhile because the materials within it were interesting to me. My interest had to carry me through many years, from proposal to completion, which it did." For Marie, a sense of purpose and ownership of the topic were crucial:

I had gone through the program once, in the late 60s, when the field was not ready for me to do what I wanted to do. So, I left school and did what was more meaningful to me. When I went back, I found things had changed. My several mentors were extremely supportive and open-minded. I never felt that I was jumping through hoops to get a union card (though if I'd stayed to finish the first time, I would have felt just that). I think my more positive experience had something to do with the fact that I really didn't care much about having a PhD...I was in school because it seemed that I could have more influence, could help more teachers and more kids, if I got the degree.

I think Tim is using the word "commitment" to describe similar feelings:

Commit yourself to your research. Grad school has evolved into the equivalent of the Shao-lin monastery for me in some respects. It has been a period of great intellectual and emotional growth, a transformation. Many times I have found myself at the end of my rope, ready to give up (needless to say, this was the entry period). If you are going to do the research, then give it everything you've got. There's no use putting yourself through the ringer if you are not ready to go all the way with it. At this point, I feel like I am ready to go back out into the world; I have passed all my tests except for one—the thesis. Somehow knowing that I have survived all the crises up to now gives me the feeling that finishing will be relatively easy. I feel like I have control. I think this is because I have followed much of the advice I have passed on to you.

QUESTIONS

8. Have you considered what it means to be "the research instrument"? How do you view yourself in relationship to your proposed focus and the people with whom you will work to investigate it? Who are you as a researcher? What do you expect from yourself and toward others?
9. Are you prepared to question yourself? Your motives? Your assumptions, values and sense of priorities? How 'close' to yourself are you willing to become?
10. How much ambiguity are you willing—and able—to handle?
11. What is, or how will you define, the nature of your relationship with your research participants? Who is responsible for defining it?
12. Might a suggested trilogy of research "Rs" be respect, responsibility, rigor? What might each imply about the ethics of the study? About your interactions within the focus and context of the study? Do you think about this?

Summary

The very nature of qualitative research links it to the human being who is the researcher. I am curious to know if researchers choosing traditional methods feel as possessive about their work as my correspondents and I do. If they do, what is the essence of that linkage, for example, person to topic? person to results? Are any of our experiences of meaning making the same? Whatever might be the case, perhaps an excerpt from one of Jean's early letters offers a fitting closure here:

Going through the doctoral process is not for the faint-hearted. You have to want it so badly that you can taste it. Having a sense of ownership of your learning and your research can certainly help you get through—sustain you—when the light at the end of the tunnel is red and the alternative tunnels seem blocked with debris.

As I reflect on Jean's comments, I am not sure <u>now</u> that in my past research I have "owned" anything; rather, the context took hold of me—we danced, but I left before the music was over. Although I ended my interaction within the immediate context, the lives of the individuals with whom I interacted dance on without me, but also within me. Some of the learning I did there has claimed <u>me</u>. I would like to suggest, therefore, that the aphorism "good things never last" is wrong; perhaps good things—by which I mean the emerging sophistication of the researcher as a thinking, feeling, interactive human being who is the research instrument—will last. What we come to 'own', then, is not the context, but our responsibility to it and our emerging ability to handle it well.

6

UNDERSTANDING BY WRITING:
Keeping a Journal

Some people keep diaries and journals as a matter of personal choice. Other people are writers, or perhaps historians or notetakers, who wish to remember particular events. During the course of thesis research, many of the correspondents found, as I did, that keeping a journal in some form was worth doing. It became a resource of our own creation and experience.

As I was organizing this book, the value of a journal seemed to go beyond the explicit commentaries of the correspondents. A journal provides a solid link to the many simultaneous levels of experience that are involved in the process of qualitative research. It can provide a place where the research focus and the role of the researcher meet methodological and analytical concerns. It can be a place to make explicit questions and concerns for later answering and organizing; a journal can hold your heart. For these reasons I decided to make "Keeping a Journal" its own chapter. I imagine this chapter as a bridge between the preceding one on focus and the subsequent one on methodology and analysis. Better yet, I think that the journal is a way of imaging a stream that flows through (underneath?) and surrounds the territory of qualitative research.

You will notice as you read that there appear to be a variety of definitions of "journal"; the question posed earlier, "What's in a name?" is an issue in this chapter. The excerpts that follow will probably not help you formulate the 'definitive' journal. They will, however, offer a number of possibilities from which you might choose.

Almost all of the correspondents responded to this topic in their letters, as I had specifically asked in my original letter, "Do/did you keep a journal?" Ann replies in the affirmative:

> Yes, I am keeping a journal. My advisor wasn't particularly impressed by my wanting to keep a journal or notes on the research process. More work. After an interview, I have at times found it tedious to write up a description of the person interviewed and the experience of what I am finding, but I have mostly enjoyed examining my navel and best of all, found it valuable to look at my notes later as I proceed with analysis.

I was delighted to find that reading the description in my journal of a woman I had interviewed two months ago really brought her to life again for me as well as the experience of interviewing her.

Later, she adds:

At first, for perhaps one month, I wrote everything up in a lined book as if I was writing a research diary. I also had separate pages taken from a separate folder in which I kept the accounts of each interview. Then I happened to reread Bogdan and Biklen (1982) and was reminded of the techniques they suggest for keeping research notes in their data analysis chapter. Based on their suggestions I now have:

1) A journal in which I write up accounts of initial contact and interviews. Beyond description, I try to include an account of what I found out in that interview, e.g., did I find anything striking? was there an image that stood out? did something a person said remind me of another interview? I make a note if there is anything I want to ask the next interviewee or if there are other ideas I should try out. I write this up directly after an interview.

2) I also have a research journal (like a diary). I write this at the end of each day. Here I try to comment or reflect on what I am learning method-wise, what I am learning substance-wise and perhaps see if I can make connections with theory. I might also have a bright idea about the way to describe something that is going on in the research.

Robert is enthusiastic about his decision to keep a journal:

I kept a journal and urge others to do so. It provides a forum from which hypotheses emerge. By reviewing accumulated data (and clutter!) one sees themes emerging. It also provides the putty to fill in holes or a basis for tossing out ideas—not enough or contradictory information to support hypotheses. In short, it was a sounding board. I reviewed mine recently and, after two years, I can still see how my thoughts proceeded from inklings to full-blown conclusions.

My own effort at keeping a journal falls somewhere between Ann's and Robert's. I did flesh out my interview interactions immediately after each interview. I wanted to be sure I remembered our interaction as I had perceived it. I added these reflections about 'fact' and 'perception' directly into my field notes, using a colored pen/pencil. Then, on the long drive home or in the solitude of the inviting guest room provided by a wonderful, intelligent, and caring couple I had only just met, I would talk into my tape recorder about everything that was going on in my head. Method combined with feelings, which combined with hunches, which combined with doubts, which combined with ideas. Back on campus, I would transcribe the tapes. Then I went through the ramblings and sorted them into their own categories. Feelings, themes, areas to probe, frustrations, etc., emerged from the 'dump'. Hence, although I can see the value in keeping two journals, I really only kept one—my field notes and my tape-recorded talk/ramblings/journal; this strategy seems natural to me.

Paula also thinks it is a good idea to keep a journal:

Yes, I kept a journal. It is like a diary with feelings and frustrations included in the entries.

There is probably a lot of insight in my journal entries. I believe that a journal is a 'must' for qualitative research studies. The journal entries acted as a catharsis, releasing my tension, renewing my spirits, and bringing to consciousness my thoughts, emotions and fears. I wrote in it during the data collection and analysis phases of my study. I went back to it during analysis to read various entries, which enabled me to draw some conclusions.

Kathryn relates that her journal was particularly useful when she began focusing on a thesis topic:

To answer your question about the journal, I think I should summarize how I came to identify my research topic. I summarized each quarter of my clinical work in a formal paper. I reconstructed this summary from the notes I kept during clinical experiences. (My program had a strong clinical orientation; I used the summaries of 20 quarter hours of clinical work to focus on my area of clinical and research interest.) So, while I really did not think of it as keeping a journal, my notes served that purpose. I also kept notes during the analysis phase of my research in order to clarify why [emphasis added] I was thinking something so I could go back later and reconstruct. What was interesting about this is sometimes I labored over these decisions and when I came back to them later, I was surprised how clear it was to me. I think keeping notes in itself forced the thought processes.

Not all correspondents had great luck with or kept journals; a few kept other kinds of supporting records. Pat writes:

I tried to keep a journal, but it was poorly done. Because I could relive the episode on tape, I did little journaling. Reflection was, more appropriately, my method of focusing my research perspective. I found that although I had spent much time in my own classroom, only when I was able to 'step around the desk' and be a part of the play did I come to know the children as human beings. My reflection forced my thinking and sent me to additional readings as I searched for those who looked at young children as part of the culture.

Patricia did not keep a journal of her experiences. Kristin's effort sounds similar to my own, "I didn't keep a journal but did write 'notes on notes' after I transcribed interviews and wrote field notes. In these notes I talked about categories emerging in the data, comparisons with the other sites, and my emotions about the fieldwork." Nancy's experience offers another option:

I did not keep a personal journal of the dissertation experience. I kept careful records while conducting my mini-case study—of my interviews, observations, etc., labeling them with date, place, actors, and any pertinent information (such as the explosion of the Challenger shuttle, which occurred during the lunch hour and just before I interviewed someone who had seen the TV report).

Gretchen responds differently by writing, "I did not keep a journal, and of course now I wish I had." In the excerpt that follows, Jean uses almost the exact same language; I remain curious as to why both of these correspondents might do things differently today:

I did not keep a journal of my process, although I wish now that I had. I kept a teaching journal and a very private journal (which I have since destroyed) at the time I was working on the dissertation, but I did not have time for a journal of my process. (I was ill during part of the time I was working on my dissertation and had to face major surgery. I kept a private journal concerning that process which I used to 'vent my spleen'. My husband was very supportive throughout everything and knew I kept that journal. He knows that it was destroyed after it had served its purpose.) I have kept the teaching journal and may use that sometime in the future in some form of research

Still another among the 20 correspondents remembers the research experience:

No, I did not keep a journal, but I did write all of these things into the text of my thesis, which is a running narrative of why decisions were made (logic, necessity, bureaucratic constraints) and of the tradeoffs I made. For example, the choice of one participant for my study was very risky, for that person had an intense crush on me and revealed it to me. I am fairly comfortable with such things, having experienced them myself, but that was one of the potential 'problems' I discussed with my advisor. It could have exploded in my face, and my degree with it. It could have been hard to be 'objective' (not quite the right word, I think, but you know what I mean). It could also have been an asset because of the nature of the openness between us, and, in fact, that was what occurred. My advisor left the decision entirely up to me, and I did exactly what I wanted to.

QUESTIONS

1. Whose decision is it to keep a journal? Yours? Your advisor's?
2. What are the advantages of keeping a journal? What are the disadvantages?
3. Is "examining one's navel" of particular benefit to qualitative researchers? If so, must the reflections be written down? Are peer debriefing or taping thoughts while driving viable alternatives?
4. "Bringing to consciousness" is one aspect of the doing–thinking–writing–discovering–understanding process that is qualitative research. Does writing force or encourage reflection, and/or does reflection enable writing?
5. Can you separate product from process? Is it important to—or not to? Why or why not?
6. Do you like to write?

Summary

An underlying theme of this book is that writing is an integral part of what qualitative research is all about. For some, keeping track of personal feelings and professional experience provides ongoing support for and confirmation of the process; however, as Maria suggests, doing so may not be for everyone. She writes, "In regard to your question about keeping a journal, my advisor encouraged all of us to do so. Some members of the Dissertation Study Group did. I must confess, I never did, and even though I came to regret it, I still cannot bring myself to keep journals on other issues I am researching."

In the few pages that follow, the journal of correspondent Helen Rolfe may provide some clues as to why Maria might regret not keeping one. Although labeled "Notes on Methodology" and included as Appendix F in her dissertation, I believe that Helen's writing offers a strong example of the multifaceted reflections a human being experiences when he or she is the research instrument within the particular context of a study. Helen has pulled examples from her field notes to highlight a variety of questions, learnings, and growing understandings of methodological issues and personal concerns. Her contribution points to the importance of notetaking and reflection during the process of qualitative research for the doctoral dissertation:

APPENDIX F
NOTES ON METHODOLOGY

As the study progressed, I had many thoughts about what was happening as I met and interviewed people in the two schools. These notes represent some themes that ran through the field notes taped after each data collection occurrence.

Emergent design. Into the study, it became apparent what 'emergent design' meant. As much as I had anticipated in the proposal, changes were inevitable once the data collection began. The research proposal, seemingly airtight and sensible when it passed the scrutiny of the committee, has been modified, trimmed, and shaped in the actual doing of this study. You cannot anticipate the events that will cause you to have to change what you have outlined to do...I have not been able to be in the schools every two weeks. My visits have been much more like monthly (field notes, 4/29/88).

Unwilling participants. One teacher was very reluctant to be taped. I persuaded her to talk with me with the tape running, with the understanding that if she was not happy, she could opt out of the study. By the end of the interview she seemed very relaxed and amenable to my coming for an observation of a lesson, a sign to me that the interview had gone well. Other cases did not end so well. It was disappointing not to have the central office coordinator participate in the study. In my haste to set up a meeting with her, I had my secretary call and make the appointment. There was a misunderstanding about my purpose for the meeting with her, and it contributed to her refusal to participate, I think.

Interview technique. Early in the study I was overcome with how hard it was to restrain myself during interviews. I had to bite my tongue several times, and I was unsuccessful other times, trying to keep from putting words in his mouth, to draw conclusions for him. It's real important that these folks have the opportunity to draw their own conclusions about what they're telling me (field notes, 2/1/88).

Sometimes the tape recorder intruded on interviews. At one point I had a strong desire to be less obtrusive with it. It would be nice to have a tape recorder that looked like an orchid, or a corsage. You just put it on and say, "Speak into the flower bud, please" (field notes, 2/29/88).

Silence is an effective technique, I found. In one interview there were several times when the person cut an answer off and then was silent. I remained silent, too. Then she added something more. I think it's important to let someone talk, even if that person is somewhat uncomfortable with the idea of talking (field notes, 3/17/88).

First interviews. At the beginning of the study in each site there was an initial awkwardness in the first interviews. I didn't have a sense of what was going on in the school. It was as though I needed to have an event or happening, some entry point, so to speak, on which to focus questions. Once I had learned something about each school, it was easier to ask about current happenings as I eased into the interviews. That I felt a need to establish a shared understanding for the context with the persons whom I interviewed is a confirmation of the groundedness of qualitative research. The fact is that knowledge of how X was implemented could not be divorced from the context in which it occurred....

The importance of viewpoint. After interviewing her, it was impressed on me that what one learns about the subject at hand depends entirely on the person to whom one is talking. The view I was shown by her of what was going on was a very different picture from the one painted by another. It contradicted in almost every way the impression the other created.

Participant's reactions. With few exceptions there was very little feedback from any participants on the transcripts of interviews throughout the study. As we talked there was almost no probing of my intent.... At the end of the study, especially at one site, participants wanted to know what I would do with the results of the data collection.

Relationship between researcher and participants. One source of bias in qualitative research occurs when the researcher identifies with the participants in the study. I was not immune to personal involvement at one of the sites. By April, 1988, my field notes report this, in passing:

> I really valued her input, because I believe in this site. I had to watch how I interacted with one or two persons, because of how easy it was to talk to them.

> She is pretty uninhibited and up front, an easy interview. So easy, you have to watch for what she doesn't say (field notes, 5/4/88).

Rigors of the methodology. It was not always easy to know what was going on. One person described what she was doing, but as I reflected on it going home, it sounded like a home-grown curriculum with little attention to learner objectives. That's the way it sounds to me. It may not be that way. But how do you know? You listen to what a person says. You ask. You look. Then you trust your instincts (field notes, 5/6/88).

People talk to you and they either (a) communicate well, giving you one impression, or (b) communicate poorly, leaving another impression. Then you observe and see (c) what people were talking about, or (d) other things, not mentioned....

There was often a piercing sense of uncertainty about what I should be doing. That feeling came to the surface in one of the last interviews, when I found myself saying aloud things I had not to that point admitted to myself. Everything I have done is something new, and I have found that I am often very much afraid. If I move to a new phase, the first thing I have to get over is the feeling that I don't want to do this, because I am afraid (1) that I don't know what to do, and (2) that I won't do it right. I have found that once I get through that, then I get in and somehow things pull together (interview, 11/11/88).

Knowing when to end. After a year's investigation of the topic it was not hard to recognize signs pointing to the end of the study. I was suddenly overcome with the feeling that there wasn't any point in my talking with him anymore. I don't have lingering questions about his views or his interpretation of events for this Fall. So I simply said, "I've just come by to ask you whether you think we need to talk again." He didn't, and I thanked him for helping me out (field notes, 12/19/88).

Analysis as an intuitive process. I suppose the process of analysis I used should be called intuitive; it was certainly not mechanical. Although throughout the study there were strong indications of themes within and across sites, the process remained a mystery, revealed only as it happened. There was no way for me to anticipate what would happen. My field notes said things like "Maybe the analysis will....Who knows?"

I constantly read and reread notes and interviews to steep myself in the information. Insights about what it meant came from somewhere, but I was never sure where. It was not difficult to support the ideas and thoughts I came up with, but they seemed to appear whole, in clusters, not piecemeal with lines attached to antecedents.

Personal feelings. I've gotten an absolutely wonderful start here. Coming home, my adrenalin was flowing. I was on a real high, because this interview today led me so quickly into what they're doing that it gives me a rich background against which to lay other perceptions of the program (field notes, 1/2/88).

I was suddenly overwhelmed with the realization that there are six weeks left. It was like a ton of bricks. That this study is going to end is overwhelming to me at this point....You're never going to get to the end of the story, especially on something as complicated as this study. I am wanting to tie up all the loose ends, and it's impossible to do. I'm having that fear of withdrawal I suppose any researcher has....I feel guilty, naturally I suppose, about not having collected more data...(field notes, 11/1/88).

I worried a lot about maintaining the confidentiality of participants. This question of maintaining confidentiality and anonymity is a vexing one. My peer debriefer did a good job of establishing a pseudonym right at the beginning. If I were going to do this again, I would do the same thing: at the initial point assign another name and use it throughout the study (field notes, 11/1/88).

I hoped the issue of confidentiality would pass with time. Will there ever come a time, say four years down the line, when these data are old enough, far enough from the immediacy of the situation so that I can go back and write a fuller picture of the implementation in these schools? Maybe a lot of that will come out in the analysis. Who knows? (field notes, 11/28/88).

One reason I believe Helen's contribution to this book is important is that she has made explicit some of the seemingly 'little' thoughts qualitative researchers have as they live and interact in the research setting. I remember how everything I did, thought, or felt seemed to be of consequence. By making her feelings and thoughts visible, that is, by sharing some of her sensemaking and subsequent insights, Helen and the other correspondents enable the neophyte researcher to have a sense of what it feels like to be engaged in the context of a study. Perhaps even more importantly, the range of experiences and interactions discussed throughout this book support the concept of multiple constructions of reality and the possibility of honing in on the nature and type of experiences that will bring more 'quality' to qualitative research. Which thoughts and insights will enhance any one individual's efforts will be up to the individual as well as those in the profession interested in pushing further and knowing more. If, indeed, we learn by doing, then the value of keeping a journal may not be appreciated until the process is close to completion. In other words, understanding aspects of present practice will be fostered in future, if not simultaneous, reflection. That we do not always 'know' or appreciate now does not mean we will not come to understand later.

7

UNDERSTANDING BY DOING:
Methodology, Analysis, and so on

Ann writes, "I agree with Bogdan and Biklen (1982), that most books on qualitative research don't write well on analysis (p.145)." I think one of the reasons Ann comments on analysis is because the processes of qualitative research are multiple; they are linked and interactive, to each other and to the human being who is the research instrument. Activities, such as reading, thinking, researching, writing, redoing, and/or rethinking and writing, do not occur in a vacuum, and they often occur simultaneously. Unlike the systematic progression of selecting a particular design and following the formulas for generating significance, the image of 'progress' in qualitative research is more like one of those crazy clocks, the hour and minute hands of which revolve sometimes clockwise, sometimes counterclockwise, sometimes together, and most often in opposition, so that movement forward is not comfortingly, logically visible. We become dizzy just watching it, and dizzy is sometimes exactly how individuals doing qualitative research for their theses feel.

Because qualitative research requires personal rather than detached engagement in the context, it requires multiple, simultaneous actions and reactions from the human being who is the research instrument. As suggested in chapter 6, writing is one way to make visible what appears to be going on. Talking into a tape recorder or with a friend/colleague is another means of "bringing to consciousness," which is partly analysis and partly enabling of the process itself. But even something as taken for granted as writing or talking has major consequences as decisions are made during the interaction of persons, method, and analysis. Personal style mingles with methodological implications; for example, how is "ownership" different from bias or subjectivity? Is there a difference? Decisions about writing, such as voice and tense, become entangled with other decisions, such as where or when does the researcher's voice come in? How much of it is 'appropriate'? Should it be there at all? Earlier excerpts from the correspondents have foreshadowed this issue. Harry Wolcott (1990) addresses questions like these in his book; others, including Colleen Larson (1992), Merry Merryfield (1992), John K. Smith (1992),

Nancy Zeller (1990), Tom Barone (1992a, 1992b, in press), and I (Meloy, 1992)
are thinking about these questions as well.

Researcher as Writer

Most of the correspondents find the interaction between writer and researcher (i.e.,
the researcher as writer, methodologist as interpreter) one of the complicating
issues of their work. Paula writes:

> One other decision rule I will address dealt with the case reporting mode. I felt
> (instinctively knew?) that my dissertation should be reported in a "scientific mode"
> (whatever that means). I wrote in a factual, organized, journalistic, day-by-day
> chronicle, reporting only facts and for the most part, omitting my feelings, thoughts,
> perceptions, and presumptions. I included my feelings, thoughts, perceptions, and
> presumptions in the summary of the case reports and in the final chapter of my
> dissertation. I wanted to report the cases in this way so that the reader could draw his
> or her own conclusions. When my major professor read the case reports, the sugges-
> tion in many instances was, "why haven't you commented on this?" or she would
> write "you should comment on this." Most of the time, I had commented on these
> areas in the summary, case findings, or final chapter. I believed (and still do believe)
> that the case report should include only events that took place. Feelings, etc., of the
> reporter/researcher belong in a separate area.

Kathy shares her struggle with the 'human' aspect of being a researcher-writer as
she was experiencing it. She writes, "I am writing a case study and was led to
believe that I should report my observations as objectively as possible. I resisted
including my reactions and wasn't sure whether analysis and discussion should or
could be a part of the narrative I was writing."

Ann, still a graduate student at the time this book went to press, expresses her
predisposition prior to finishing the dissertation. She says, "Having spent some
time, energy and enjoyment collecting interview data, I would like it to be reported
richly and fully with limited academic cutback between what they say and I say.
Such a style puts qualitative data in a supporting role and makes it rather dry."

Speaking of "academic cutback," in my own notes about the writing of this book
I asked myself numerous questions, particularly after the first round of reviews
suggested I needed to put more of 'me' into it. The questions included: "Whose
voice is this anyway?"; "What is the purpose of any book? This book?"; "What are
the readers expecting? a meaning?" ; "How do you open up the possibilities for
meanings rather than converge on 'the' point?" Until qualitative researchers (who
are writers?) are able to articulate the possibilities for reading within their texts and
readers of qualitative studies are experienced in expecting these possibilities, the
former are going to have to provide some explicit guides to sensemaking. Paula
has done so in the excerpt given earlier, and Ann offers an additional perspective.
Perhaps decisions regarding voice, purpose, and meaning are less explicitly stated
in qualitative dissertations; perhaps they are indicative of analysis, existing in part

as embedded form and structure? I am beginning to think the value of these letters, issues, and concerns is that the correspondents are writing about decisions they made in order to share, in written form, the 'whole' as a meaningful context; whether that is the research context, the dissertation or both, I am not sure. Since listening to Elliot Eisner (April, 1993) give the presidential address at the American Educational Research Association (AERA), I am also thinking that any sense of 'meaning' as being able to be converged upon by number or sentence (i.e., it is there in some concise form to be underlined or abstracted), is not the point of a qualitative research project or any kind of 'qualitative' experience.

QUESTIONS

1. What is your writing style? How will you express the intermingling of you, the researcher, with the context of your study? What choices/models are available to you? What is appropriate? Acceptable? Why?
2. Which choices/models do you prefer? Which can you defend? Does 'paradigm' influence your decision here? Why or why not? Do any of the correspondents' styles 'seem right' to you? Why?
3. What are your goals for the dissertation? Do you know? Will articulating what you expect from yourself support your decision making and refine your methodological approach and analyses?
4. What do you want to 'show' in/through/by your thesis? Will or can your writing style facilitate your purposes? Who is your audience? Will that matter?

Nancy's thesis, *A Rhetoric for Naturalistic Inquiry*, poses an argument for ways to write up qualitative research:

The most important section of my dissertation, I feel, is the demonstration chapter (Chapter V). It contains some writing samples, e.g., illustrating scene-by-scene construction, use of dialogue, and detailing of status life indicators—these are relatively harmless writing techniques. I also argue that the use of the third person subjective point of view takes the writer a step toward fiction and, while very effective (e.g., see Tom Wolfe's *The Right Stuff*), can leave the researcher open to criticism regarding trustworthiness. For the same reason, the interior monologue and creation of composite characters are not writing techniques that I would recommend for researchers, especially doctoral candidates needing to please the limited readership of his/her committee.

Nancy's continued thinking, reading, and writing about writing since the completion of her thesis has also led her to revise some of her conclusions. She writes:

Regarding Chapter VI of my thesis, "An Act of Discovery"—I've been thinking a lot lately about the inherent dangers of doing and writing qualitative research. To this end, I obtained a copy of the Judith Stacey article "Can there be a feminist ethnography?" and have been editing the relevant section in Chapter VI of my dissertation ("Limitations of the Proposed Rhetoric for Naturalistic Inquiry").

Although the dissertation study will have an end point, the thinking and interacting with the thoughts and material that the experience generates will probably not. Novice qualitative researchers want some help in understanding what is possible and acceptable. As Kathy reflects, a finite conception about the processes of qualitative research would have been useful:

> Writing takes time. I still don't know how you determine the degree of detail to include in descriptions. I was asked that by one committee member. I tried writing a draft of a results or findings chapter and reacted to the feedback I got from the three people who read it. I would have welcomed information on writing the dissertation and the possibilities/options that exist. I know that those possibilities only exist if they are approved by the doctoral committee, but a chapter on the range of possibilities might help students and committee members as well.

Gretchen writes that she, too, desired some methodological support for doing qualitative research. She comments, "Developing a coding scheme, complete with rules for interpretation of categories, was something where I wished for more input from my committee, but none of them had much experience in this area."

For the qualitative researcher, doing research is synonymous with multiple, simultaneous actions. The researcher as human instrument is a methodologist, analyst, writer, thinker, interpreter, inquirer—an individual human being capable of and responsible for some kind of final, organized presentation of the interaction of experience in context. Is it any wonder that chapters on analysis are difficult to compose? Paula recalls how she organized her writing:

> The organizational format I used included numbering each paragraph of the case reports (much like a legal document) and referencing these paragraphs when I discussed the case findings. This format aided me in two ways: (1) It helped me maintain an exemplary audit trail. I found the audit trail especially helpful during rewrites, when I omitted paragraphs and parts of paragraphs in an effort to improve the case reports; I didn't want the final case report to look like a data dump. (2) The reader could more readily see the reason for my finding statements. In other words, I documented my findings. It was worth the effort. BY NOW I GUESS YOU CAN SEE THAT I AM A VERY ORGANIZED PERSON![3]

QUESTIONS

5. Have you looked at any dissertations for examples of style? Have you read any of the current literature dealing with the writing of qualitative research,

---

[3]The concept of an audit trail (Halpern & Schwandt, 1988; Lincoln & Guba, 1985) supports the logical documentation of the evolution (not necessarily logical!) of the thesis.

or read research articles describing or exemplifying it? Is the writing as important as the substance/ results/hypotheses/interpretations? Why or why not?

6. Which, if any, writing techniques are expected in your dissertation document? Which reference format? Are voice and tense already mandated? How will you find out?

7. Are you familiar with audit trail techniques? Computer sorting/coding packages? Are you a detail-oriented person? If not, can anything discussed in this book so far support your qualitative research efforts? If so, what are the 'logical' choices for you? Why?

Qualitative and Quantitative

Concepts from scientific research remain prime target areas of concern for the doctoral student who may have to answer questions about generalizability, bias, and validity, for example. Gretchen recalls:

> My committee was happy with my statement that field studies have limited generalizability.... Reviewers for journals such as the *NCA Quarterly*, *Communication Studies*, and *Human Communication Research* have been less kind; they have criticized my submitted articles for the lack of generalizability.

Kathryn remembers being concerned about this issue as well:

> In the methods chapter I devoted a good deal of paper to description of the sample and included more in the appendix. I described typical and atypical courses of illness. I included as much data as I thought would convey to doubters that these individuals were coping with serious illness; the "rich description" rule became very important because my sample was nonrandom.

> I clearly stated my position on generalizability:

>> "The acute myocardial infarction (AMI) patients interviewed in this study seem representative of AMI patients in general and those described in other studies. However, extensive descriptive information is provided because the sampling method was nonrandom. These descriptive data may enable potential readers to examine the fit between this study sample and any other sample for which the findings might apply (Kirk & Miller, 1986; Le Compte & Goetz, 1982; Lincoln & Guba, 1985; Sandelowski, 1986)." (pp. 35–36)

> I addressed the issue of sample size as follows:

>> "The criteria more often identified for determining appropriate sample size in qualitative research is sampling to the point of redundancy or the point at which continued inquiry reveals no new data. Experience with the pilot study suggested a priori that a sample of 30 would assure encountering this redundancy phenomenon." (p. 36)

In the excerpt that follows, Jean raises a different issue surrounding the sample. She also shares her thinking around other methodological issues:

> I had to go through the "Human Subjects Review Panel" at the University but did not have any problems, because the authors I studied had made appropriate legal arrangements with the collection about their works. I had to have letters from them and the collection bound within the pages of the dissertation. These letters were enough for the University, but University Microfilms had other ideas. I have just spent the last three months getting additional documentation to suit them....

She continues:

> I believe that there is a tie or link between the way in which naturalistic inquiry is conducted and whether or not it is perceived as easy or rigorous....If the structure is sloppy and the elements of a well-organized study are not present or poorly or improperly carried out, the study becomes suspect—even if the writing is of Pulitzer Prize quality. I look for elements such as: the establishment of and continual work at trustworthiness, triangulation, how initial and continued entrance, confidentiality, and anonymity are handled; whether field journals are kept and their condition; whether an audit trail is maintained; whether a member check has been provided for and used; etc. I think if a researcher conducting naturalistic inquiry doesn't consider such elements, then the resulting research may be viewed with suspicion....

And she adds:

> I believe that statistics, because they are one step back from people who create or generate them, are somehow viewed as 'cleansed' and free of bias. Statistics, by their very nature and definition, have been stripped of context and appear somehow 'cleaner'. (The woman from the Graduate School at my college may be 'getting by' at her university because her study is statistical in nature. The subjects of her study might be viewed as numbers and not people.) Mishler (1986) cites Cicourel ("Interviews, Surveys, and the Problems of Ecological Validity" in *American Sociologist, 17*) when he asks, "Do our instruments capture the daily life conditions, opinions, values, attitudes, and knowledge base of those we study as expressed in their natural habitat?" (p.24). Mishler and Cicourel are discussing issues surrounding research interviewing, but I believe that question should be addressed by every researcher and asked of every study.

QUESTIONS

8. Do you know the major research journals in your field? Have you examined their contents over the last 5 years for trends and exemplars? Where are things changing (e.g., topics)? What seems to remain the same? Will either of these last two questions influence the final presentation of your material? Your choice of focus and methodology? Why or why not? Can you afford to be—are you expected to be—"cutting edge" with your thesis?

9. What do you know about the Human Subjects Review Panel at your university? Where are you getting your information?
10. What do you need to know about the graduate school's requirements for ANYTHING related to the appearance and substance of your thesis? What other questions might you ask of someone there?
11. What do all these thoughts on writing have to do with methods and analysis? Has reading the excerpts from the correspondents enabled you to see how some qualitative researchers make sense of things? Do any of their strategies make explicit to you the kinds of thinking and decision making that are a part of analysis?
12. Can you define, early on, whose expectations you are to meet? Who will your audience be? Does reading these letters help you to begin to shape your own sense of direction, give voice to your own needs and concerns, and highlight where you are already 'A-OK'?
13. How rigorous is your study? By whose standards? What models? Which examples?
14. Do you have some understanding of the ramifications of your decision making around writing, methodological, and analysis issues? For example, is generalizability an issue for you? Will you change? Will journals change? What are the tradeoffs? What is important?

Data Collection and Analysis

Several correspondents, including Ann in the excerpt that follows, comment on the technical aspects of data collection:

> The ideal method would have been to videotape, but there was no way to do so without intruding on the process I was examining; also due to confidentiality concerns, permission would not have been given for videotaping. Even with audiotape, some subjects were reluctant to participate.

> This was planned as a multi-method study: content analysis of tape recordings, coding of double interacts, observation of the communication process (including nonverbal communication), and follow-up interviews.

Pat describes how her study evolved and was recorded:

> The chairperson of my committee and the department head permitted the study to move forward 'over time'. My study involved analyzing kindergarten block play throughout the school year. Video tape was accumulated at the beginning, middle, and end of the school year. No interviewing was done of the participants, but informal discussions were undertaken with parents to determine where the different topics came from that appeared in the dramatic play. The committee's concern was if I could get permission from the school district and if I would manage the technical gathering of the data.

The analysis reflected my understanding of children and what I 'saw' on the video tape. The themes and categories I 'named' truly emerged from the video tape and required the 'grouping' of like aspects into the category. I am proud to say that no tables appear in my dissertation. To support the selected categories, I used direct quotations from the episodes which are a sequential reporting of the taped block play. (I developed a typology of block play and drew from 6 episodes the extent of block play found in this group. No two episodes used the same format, however, there was demonstrated consistency in some aspects of block play across episodes.)

Robert remembers his committee's concern with his chosen methodological framework:

I found that my chosen methodologies bore the most scrutiny from my committee. They appeared satisfied with the research design once I convinced them of its rigor. The appendix of my dissertation is loaded with evidence showing: interview questions and responses; the number of times each question was asked; observed teaching (using a Hunter-based observation tool); principal behavior; and other data to provide detailed information about the school and the community. Tapes, written logs, and journals have been retained in my files. This detailed collection helped to silence the question, how much is enough?

Robert also describes his sampling procedure:

Selecting the school to be studied required the use of quantitative data. Some committee members objected to using two test results, so I incorporated question-naires (sent to area school administrators, teachers and IU directors) requesting their impressions of the schools under consideration for the study. I also used a state survey to elicit teachers' opinions of their own school. The thoroughness of the selection process satisfied the committee.

Ann's reflections, with which I began this chapter, remain critical of the distance from text to experience:

As I am doing my research, I have a better idea of my analytical process. I have found Bogdan and Biklen's (1982) analysis chapter very helpful and reassuring if I start worrying again about the 'right' answer and choosing themes and categories. They suggest—'follow some sensible organization'; the themes/questions of my question-naire are proving to be very helpful categories. Also, I'm very glad I spent a good deal of time thinking about what exactly I wanted to find out and organized quite a structured interview, although I resisted this at first.

At first glimpse, it might appear that Ann has a totally a priori focus, which is incompatible with qualitative research. You may recall, however, that Ann under-took a pilot study during which her focus became more clear in her own mind. At a certain point, qualitative researchers must determine what they are and are not doing. During the interaction of method and analysis, converging on a focus and making subsequent decisions to support that choice appears to be a common sensemaking strategy. Jane found that returning to the texts while engaged in field research is helpful. She writes:

> It has been very useful to go back to various methods books now, as I work on data analysis. Although I had read them before, tidbits are much more meaningful now that I'm into it. I guess that's true of any learning: it's meaningful when applied to a context. The advice and examples in methods books are reassuring and sometimes provide direction. Lincoln and Guba's (1985) *Naturalistic Inquiry* has been more helpful to me now than previously, when I was just learning about the methods. I really appreciate their humor, e.g., the first 90% of the project takes 90% of the time; the last 10% takes the other 90%.

> I had thought I would be farther along by now; evidently that's typical of such studies. But then again, I experience that emotional roller coaster and sometimes think, "I am in good shape! It's really moving now!"

> I was frustrated earlier this summer because I thought I could whip out the introduction, methods and lit review chapters, but I found I couldn't complete them until I had gotten into data analysis. Now I realize for me that's appropriate and OK. Because I've done some analysis, my focus is clearer and that will improve those preliminary chapters.

Carol describes her experience with 'analysis' a little differently:

> I interviewed my subjects, taped all of the interviews, transcribed them, and then mailed the transcripts back to those interviewed to have them check for content and meaning. Then I sat and looked at the transcripts for a long time. It was a hot summer in 1988! Eventually, I was able to identify some common themes. These were described as 'emerging themes'....At the end of analyzing the transcripts and identifying the emerging themes, I invited those interviewed to meet with me and review them together. About ½ of them responded. This provided another check on my perceptions.

Jean, even after finishing, could not quite put her finger on how things came together for her, a feeling reminiscent of some of Helen's comments at the conclusion of chapter 6:

> Are you familiar with Louise Rosenblatt's (1978) *The Reader, the Text, the Poem*, in which she argues for the transactional view of language? Her work certainly influenced my study. I am not sure how the themes emerged. I looked for what appeared to be common themes within both writers and their papers. The writing process as defined and discussed by Graves, Smith, Calkins, Murray and others has between three and four 'stages'. I used a variation on those stages in examining the papers, so I had a structure. I also knew that I wanted to look at the writers' lives as well as their works, so that also added to the structure.

The question of rigor is concomitant with chapters on methodology and analysis. The books listed in chapter 4 address methodological and analysis issues such as trustworthiness, dependability, and 'validity'. As of this writing, thinkers and practitioners of qualitative research have made some strong statements in regard to these issues, but the questions surrounding them are far from resolved.[4] I do think the correspondents are, implicitly and explicitly, stressing the importance of understanding the methodological choices that doctoral students and their committees make. Acquiring a solid background in qualitative research methodologies can only support your decision making.

QUESTIONS

15. Analysis is still difficult to explicitly articulate. How much ambiguity are you willing to live with? Do you trust your own abilities to think, relate, connect, resift, reconsider, change? How much support will you require from your committee? From others?
16. What ethical issues are embedded in all that has been shared so far? What does being the research instrument mean? Can you separate 'you' from the context? Why or why not? What are the implications of your choices?
17. Are any of the correspondents' suggestions useful? What sense of the qualities of the qualitative are you deriving?

Summary

As Jane pointed out earlier, understanding may only come about while doing. Books and practice each inform and enrich the other. Novice qualitative researchers seem to depend on their experience, the texts, and other people as they gain confidence in grasping the complexity of the task of writing a qualitative dissertation. At some point, they must share what they are doing with their committee. Several correspondents wrote about the interaction with their committees during the data collection and analysis phase of their studies; some frustrations are clearly expressed:

> It would have helped if I or my major professor would have clarified the relationship that should exist between me and the committee members while collecting and analyzing data and while writing the study. I assumed it was up to me and my major professor to plod along. We met regularly. I gave other committee members a draft of the first four chapters and received feedback immediately from one of the four. I never knew how actively or persistently I should seek their feedback. They all were so busy. When the second committee member responded with comments almost three months later, I felt that I was being asked to reevaluate my data, my questions, and the way I had been working during that time period. It appears that these relationships

---

[4]See back issues of the *Educational Researcher*, or Eisner & Peshkin's (1990) *Qualitative Inquiry in Education: The Continuing Debate*, and Guba's (1990) *The Paradigm Dialog*.

differ from place to place and among departments. My goal is to finish draft one this weekend and revisions next weekend. I will respond about defending this masterpiece when I am finished with that phase. Thanks for caring about us. This is an incredible learning process. I did not anticipate the emotional reactions that often are linked to exhaustion and being a 44 year old woman. Everything seems to take longer than anticipated. I finally gave up estimating and started pushing harder.... Enough for now. I am returning to Chapter 9. Pulling it all together is difficult, too. I have discovered so many interesting questions in the process of looking closely. I am convinced that qualitative studies are worth doing. I am not sure I believe the traditional dissertation format, our rite of passage to the community of scholars, is necessary. I probably would have benefitted just as much from writing a report to the coordinators of the project I studied and two articles either collaboratively with them or with input from the participants I studied. Perhaps I am just tired and looking for an easier way out.

Another correspondent reflects:

I have no evidence that anyone on the committee fully read my dissertation until about three weeks before I defended. My advisor was away for the summer and though I sent him chapters weekly, as we had agreed, he never sent them back and never commented on them until he returned. Probably he had read them and thought they were okay. I couldn't tell. He never communicated with me. (It's a good thing I was fairly confident.) When he got back into town, he read the whole thing and said it was fine, that it was time to stop writing.

Just as we are individuals, so too, then, will the questions, concerns, decisions and outcomes of our studies reflect our individual educations and interactions. Providing support for making wise choices based on a solid understanding of qualitative research methodologies is what all the books I have seen on qualitative research are attempting to do.

8

UNDERSTANDING BY FINISHING:
Defining "The End"

Defining the end is not easy, as we are never, in an absolute sense, quite there. Although most of the correspondents expressed relief at being finished, several chose to write in some detail about bringing closure to the dissertation experience. The issues they addressed include publication concerns and working with and through the graduate school. I have chosen to close this chapter with Kathy's reflective summation of points salient to her and another correspondent's story of ending.

Publication

If I am understanding the ramifications of the correspondents' thoughts that follow, perhaps publication concerns need to be addressed much earlier in the research process, perhaps even prior to methods and focus. The question of audience, which was addressed in the earlier chapters of this book, reappears in more detail:

> The dissertation has yielded several convention papers but so far no publications. The articles including no quantitative tables have been rejected outright from the scholarly journals in my field. Those which have focused on the last minute, a priori hypotheses have rated 'revise and submit' letters. I am still in the process of reworking and resubmitting or sending to other journals.

> I am presently an assistant professor in my third year. If I am to be considered for tenure, I need to have a minimum of 6 or 7 research articles published in high quality academic journals. At times I find myself wishing I had chosen a quantitative project for my dissertation. Although editorial policies state an interest in both quantitative and qualitative studies, they do not yet accept many qualitative studies in my field.

Jean reflects about publication and rejection from a different perspective:

> I have hopes of publishing two chapters from my dissertation as separate books....I have presented some of my data in the form of a paper...which will be published in

the proceedings' volume. I have written a couple of pieces as a result of that effort. They are 'making the rounds'. Perhaps because one of the participants in my study is somewhat controversial (which was one of the reasons I was drawn to this person), a couple of the major journals in the field have been reluctant to consider the articles....

Kathy poses some questions relevant to the writing of the dissertation. They reflect some of the concerns highlighted in earlier chapters, specifically, for whom is the dissertation being written?

All of the dissertations I read followed the five chapter quantitative format. This is different from the style and format developing in the reports of qualitative studies in journal articles and books.

Should the models be changing as we continue to explore possibilities? I read recently that many dissertations are being written using the style and format of manuscripts and articles that can be submitted for publication. Is this happening in colleges of education? Or do the rules regarding form and style we impose on dissertations create documents for our committee members and other doctoral students looking for models or possibilities?

I have a hunch that the continuing efforts doctoral students choosing to use qualitative research for their theses make will have a major impact on the "rules regarding form and style." As a doctoral student, you are in a unique position of learning and understanding. You may be working alone or with your peers and committee. Most importantly, perhaps, you are actively engaged in seeking answers to your questions about theory and practice. Reflecting and writing about those questions can direct you and others toward possible answers.

Endings

Almost 9 months after the 1991 Qualitative Research in Education conference, Kathy sent me a brief letter highlighting dissertation experiences that she found most memorable. As I read the letter, I thought that it brought a sense of closure to the experience of doing thesis research in general and qualitative research in particular. The paragraphs that follow might as easily be written as "bullets" and titled "Tips for the Qualitative Researcher"; they could easily have introduced this book as well:

The enclosed notes were written in July when I was cleaning out files; I had scribbled on the pad that you might be interested in having them? Here goes.

Pay attention to responses you give when people ask what your dissertation is about. Every response refines and clarifies the important findings and relationships.

I found that I drew diagrams and illustrations on a pad when I met with my advisor, but I failed to date these scribbled illustrations. These were important steps in formulating an organizational schema, but I didn't realize it.

Regular conferences with your major professor, co-researchers, etc., are important. I've read that regular conferences are important for analytic and psychological security. I agree.

I wish I would have dated articles I copied and read along the way. I would recommend dating everything and keeping a notebook handy at all times.

Driving provides an opportunity for thinking and analyzing categories, relationships, etc. Metaphors seem to come to mind while driving places, or running. The danger is that one's head becomes so occupied with thoughts and possibilities that traffic violations are common among doctoral students—speeding, running stop signs, failing to renew drivers' licenses. I was surprised to learn that I was not alone when I began to compare occurrences with others.

I also cried a lot during the year I was working on my dissertation. I blamed it on being 40 something, but I learned that fellow graduate students in their twenties and thirties cried a lot. I was at a meeting one day when I was overtired and started crying when asked to do a small task. People apologized for things that had not offended me. I just couldn't envision one more thing to do on top of the dissertation deadlines that I felt I couldn't meet. Everything seemed to take longer than I anticipated.

There needs to be a stopping point. Analysis and refining diagrams can go on indefinitely and there is so much data, so many interesting tidbits to explore in this type of study.

Preparing to defend a qualitative study requires simplifying findings and presenting highlights. Expect the unexpected. The questions asked and comments made validate the importance of qualitative studies. Committee members react to different occurrences and details. The readers take away what is pertinent to them.

I was disappointed that I didn't get enough feedback from committee members during my defense. I didn't realize that the defense also marked the end of the doctoral program and my relationship with people I respected. I wanted more from them than the structure of the defense allowed. I wasn't sure what my role during the defense should be. Could I have redirected questions or asked questions of committee members or was my role solely to respond, to explain and clarify?

It is over! I graduated and the copies are being bound. I became a better writer in the process and continuously appreciated the complexity of human interactions and of schooling. The word dilemma took on new meaning. Dilemmas were a part of my life.

Kathy's letter portrays, perhaps, a traditional way to image "the end." We look back on our experience and recall the peaks and valleys. Another perspective on the end requires one to conceptualize the entire process of doing a qualitative dissertation as enabling an individual to get 'there'; imaging the hurdles of ambiguity can enable the novice qualitative researcher to adjust his or her stride. The questions, concerns, and issues that are answered, solved, or avoided become particles of the final whole.

Few correspondents even mentioned their final defense. But as one correspondent relates in the story that follows, all of the aphorisms about finishing (e.g., it's not over 'til it's over; it's not over 'til the fat lady sings) need to be carefully heeded. Defending the end is <u>not</u> the same as finishing:

AFTER THE DEFENSE

The Politics of the Graduate School

My story begins only after the defense had taken place. My committee signed off on the dissertation and I was left—alone, literally—to negotiate the dissertation's acceptance with the Graduate School. The excitement of the completion of the defense was rudely tempered with the problems the Graduate School presented. It was as if I entered a 'different game' with new players or rules with no support or assistance from my committee or the School of Education. I did not know that the 'General' existed within the Graduate School who would manipulate me further. I thought the 'war' had been won once the defense had been completed. I was to learn a 'new' lesson.

My department had had only one qualitative dissertation go through the Graduate School (only 5 dissertations in all) less than eight weeks before mine, and it had been difficult. My co-chair advised me to use a 'particular' typist to complete the job. I had initially resisted the suggestion thinking I could do it myself. (I viewed myself as able to type, use the computer and spell check, and knowledgeable enough of the required style format to accept the corrections which might come from the reader; money, of course, was a major concern.)

I came to understand why using 'this' typist was so important as the final drafts of chapters were re-worked. I became unable to see the need for corrections and the revisions were very slow to complete. I had worked with the copy so long that I was unable to read what was written, and often would read what I thought was there on the page.

My typist was an individual who knew the style format and the Graduate School staff like the back of her hand. She had been used as a typist by many others within the University complex and was well-respected. She worked in a medical lab and was very good at cleaning up and clearing up jargon that made the text less than clear while knowing/appreciating different dissertation formats. She enjoyed the type of dissertation I presented to her. She not only typed the text but also edited the final product.

This typist told me repeatedly how helpful I was with what I brought to her, and how easy the job would be to complete. She often told me not to worry. It must have been obvious how nervous I was, as once again I felt 'powerless' because I had to rely on others for assistance in the completion of the dissertation.

What happened, is that I found myself re-negotiating my dissertation with the Graduate School staff acting as the final decision maker. This Graduate School staff was a single decision maker, a secretary, who followed the traditional 5 chapter format approach. Having my typist, however, gave me 'insider' status, because she was seen as 'one of their own'. I had only to mention her name and possible questions or problems seemed to be manageable. When I turned in the first draft, I was asked to supply the name of the typist. When I gave her name, I was reassured that there would probably be no problem.

My first problem had to do with the transcripts of my data which my committee had required me to include as an appendix. My committee had felt it was important for others to have access to the transcripts from which my categories came. The presentation was not initially acceptable to the Graduate School, i.e., the secretary. For example: The Graduate School did not like the printer I used for my data (transcripts). They wanted the entire transcription of my data to be re-typed to be consistent with the remainder of the document. My typist said it was not necessary as it was "raw data." The style manual does not call for raw data to be presented in such a format since they were to appear as an appendix. (I did not check this fact. My typist's matter-of-fact response led to a telephone exchange with the Graduate School. She commanded enough power within the Graduate School to let this aspect of my appendices be reported as they originally appeared...saving me some money, which was my typist's point in "calling the secretary's hand.")

I finished in August, the very busiest time for the Graduate School. The outside person selected to read my dissertation was only used in cases when everyone else was busy. This reader did not understand her job; she edited the format I chose, which was different from the standard 5 chapter design, by making remarks that indicated to me she did not understand qualitative research. There was no problem with the references, grammar or spelling, but over and over in the document she used her green pen to remark: "WHY IS THIS HERE AGAIN? I'VE READ THIS BEFORE?" Receiving the manuscript for corrections, I could not believe that page after page would have something circled or crossed out that had nothing to do with grammar, spelling or citation reference. I was furious! I took the 'box' (containing the dissertation) back to my typist, who was as upset as I was. She told me that this reader was not often used, and she would make a call to the Graduate School. (It cost me another $50.00 to recover the material which had been marred by her green pen. This did not include the transcript appendix in which the reader continued to question, marking with green pen.)

...My final run-in with the Graduate School involved the page numbering which was out of sequence by the end of all this. The office had looked over the dissertation 4 times and had not caught it. At this late date, they were asking me to rework the dissertation because I had two pages numbered 104. I refused. I asked to speak to the Dean. I was denied personal or phone access. He told the Graduate School to "take care of it." My point was simply after 4 proofs, it was not my problem. Page numbering had never been identified as "needed correction." The secretary gave up and numbered the pages 104 and 104b.

From all these experiences occurring during an eight week period, I have learned that using the techniques of qualitative research to complete the dissertation process are helpful. My typist was an "informant." I would probably still be negotiating with the Graduate School if she had not been part of my 'team'. (It must be mentioned that my committee all went on vacation after my defense. I hope no one else has a story sequence like mine. I learned so much about 'the system' completing my dissertation, it's a wonder I want to work in higher ed.!)

It has taken me several sittings at the computer to write this to you. Although it has been nearly nine months since these events occurred, I still get upset reliving them. Maybe someone else could benefit from the story of the typist who could walk the mine field.

Defining the end is something a qualitative researcher is only in the position to do <u>at</u> the end (rather than at a proposal hearing, chapter checkpoints, etc.), when it is finally able to be constructed from the interaction of the researcher with context. Some of our methodologies, strategies, and perhaps even contexts may compare across researches. But the interactions of person with context, researcher with researched, human being with him or herself and among others, and the dynamic of the individual as writer, analyzer, and interpreter are integrated and often simultaneous; they are human and concern us as individuals. They can be made explicit and shared.

Perhaps that is why I am not so sure that the story just given and Kathy's letter should not appear in the first chapter of this book. Although we are accustomed to beginning at the beginning, defining the possibilities and problems of endings might help us better prepare for the trip ahead, which is the idea with which this book began. It is not a new idea; I think Aesop probably had it in mind a long time ago, as have most of our grandparents and even ourselves (i.e., we can and do learn from the experiences of others). Although we consider it crucial that the author of the story get 'the' point(s) across, what we, the readers/listeners <u>choose or are able to learn</u> from the described experience is, in part, up to us.

Learning with and through others is a fundamental quality of the qualitative. The level of analysis of 'war stories' is not purely the acceptance/rejection of thick description; the description can, for example, provide insights into possible interpretations of action, examples of experiences to either seek out or avoid, as well as simply increase the awareness of the possibilities within a particular context. As a result, a novice inquirer and faculty or family member can grasp the ambiguities of context and process inherent in the pursuit of the doctorate by means of qualitative research. In addition, those of us committed to pushing our understandings of the 'qualities of the qualitative' can use such commentaries on experiencing to provoke our thinking on issues critical to responsible and humane research.

9

BEGINNING WITH ENDINGS

Although several reviewers and friends all stated that there needed to be more of 'me' in this book, I am convinced that there was plenty of me here before I made so many explicit comments and connecting statements. Is qualitative research about the context, or is it about the researcher, who defines the needle, spins the thread, and pieces together the understandings? I have a diagram in my notes; there is a line = arrow = the researcher directed toward a bull's eye = target = context. The perspective from the tip of the arrow prior to entering the field (the arrow lined up to the target from 100 yards away) looks different than the target from the tip of the arrow immersed in the context. At some point, the arrow is removed from or falls out of the context, and again, the perspective from the tip changes. As Joseph Heller's (1974) book title suggests, *Something Happened*. Qualitative researchers leave their mark not only in the context but also on any resulting documentation and discussions. Not only are they learning about a particular context, but they are also learning from and with it. Meaning is mobile, transitory, and cumulative.

I know very little about literary criticism, but I have read essays and previewed books that attempt to get at the <u>one</u> meaning behind Joyce or Updike, Fowles or Shakespeare. I was brought up in an age where symbolic interpretation of literature was in vogue. I will never forget my failed attempt to waive the freshman basic composition class requirement because I could not decide if the poem was symbolic or meant to be read only on an explicit level. The author of that poem visited my campus in the fall of my freshman year; he laughed at all of us who chose to interpret his poem as being about anything other than exactly what was written. I had been taught to look for 'hidden' meaning; I was in freshman composition because I had not seen the author's meaning there before me. No, that is not quite accurately stated: I remember having 'seen' it; I simply found a different one. And you may, too. Although I believe I have expressed my intentions from the beginning, the following is an attempt to suggest some of the more explicit possibilities:

- I mean this book to be supportive in ways I cannot be to people whom I may never meet. There are emerging cohorts of individuals who support each other's and the neophyte's attempts at doing qualitative research. I wrote this book in hopes of being a part of these efforts.

- I also mean this book to provoke questions; I have heard others ask many of the ones written down here. I think sharing some answers—or the possibilities of better questions—is useful for us at this time in the history of inquiry. I mean to expose (rather than resolve) issues, concerns, and problems that face doctoral students, their families, and committee members.
- I mean this book to be a contribution, not to determining 'the' meaning of thinking about and doing qualitative research for one's thesis, but to the thinking about and doing of qualitative research in general.

As I traced the issues running throughout the pages of this book, I noted the following themes:

- Limited opportunities for some graduate students to learn about qualitative research and the limitations of some learning.
- The complexity and ambiguity surrounding the multiple, simultaneous processes of doing qualitative research and being the research instrument.
- Qualitative researchers are decision makers and sense makers; they are—or become—writers.
- There are implicit and explicit power relations surrounding the formulating, doing, and reporting of qualitative research for the dissertation.
- Learning occurs by reading, doing, talking, sharing, feeling, writing, and reflecting.
- Qualitative dissertations/research appear to represent attempts at expressing a 'whole' of experience.

I cannot say "in conclusion..." because I am probably at yet another beginning, laden with some thoughts that had not occurred until the organizing, writing, and editing of this book. Some of the thoughts are laced throughout this book; I am uncertain now if they are mine, the correspondents', ours, or perhaps even yours. However, I am certain that determining ownership may be less important than the idea that the thoughts themselves offer support for doing qualitative research to those who will undertake it. "How to" books will tell us what to do and which rules to follow. Experience will guide us in minute ways that the books have not yet made clear. Colleagues, peers, and co-learners will push the levels of understanding in order to clarify possible meanings—for future researchers and researches. I mean to help foster understanding by continuing to try to do so.

APPENDIX A:
Original Letter to Potential Correspondents

JUNE 1990

Dear

Thank you for responding to my request. In the next few paragraphs, I will provide the context of a situation I would like your help remedying!!! If that sounds too "a priori," please indulge me just a little.

As I was trying to write up my dissertation, I had several difficulties. First, the case study method did not seem appropriate for the study I undertook. Second, because I had a 'quantitative' committee with the exception of Egon Guba (I was his graduate assistant for two years at Indiana University), I had at least two competing approaches for the structuring of my effort! Several 'conflicts' had to be argued and sorted through, including:

- The question of voice—1st or 3rd person;
- The question of conceptual framework—
  an emergent design based on a general focus, or
  a priori hypotheses;
- The question of the literature review—
  to provide the arena for thinking/
  to be useful/located throughout the thesis, or
  to establish the 'problem';
- The question of methods—
  is an 'n=8' enough?
  what kind of interview IS that?
  where are the a priori categories for your
  respondents (asst/full prof., etc.)?
- The question of analysis—
  how do you know if you've got the 'right' answers?

why did you pick those themes/categories?
how did you come up with those tables?
how will you report the data? how will you select
   quotes/vignettes, etc.?
where are your conclusions?

There were other questions and memorable interactions among my committee members as we attempted to negotiate the structure and format of the dissertation. I need your help in answering these and other questions, such as:

1. What did you have to negotiate with your committee?
2. What decision rules guided the formulation of your thesis, i.e., My dissertation looks like this because...
3. What does the final form of your dissertation look like? Did you follow a particular format, such as Yin's case study method? or is it a "traditional" dissertation, with 4/5 chapters Kerlinger would recognize?
4. How, or did you deal with the assumptions about the inquiry? (questions of the nature of truth, objectivity, value, generalizability?) What were those assumptions? How did you deal with "validity" and "reliability" issues? Which texts/authors provided the basis of your decisions?
5. Did you keep a journal? Would there be any insights about the formulation of your effort from which others might learn? Questions or decisions about what you did and why you did it...including intuition, necessity, etc.!

It is my plan to compile and analyze the information you return to me and present it in a small book. I think a book dealing with these decision 'rules' would be valuable to individuals who are beginning to take a serious look at qualitative inquiry. I also believe that 'quantitative' committee members might benefit from the concerns each of us has addressed. Finally, I think a thoughtful effort around this topic would save many of us time, in that some decisions have been made with adequate, and accepted, justifications.

I am presently an assistant professor of education at Castleton State College in Castleton, Vermont. I have also served as an evaluation consultant for the Connecticut State Department of Education and as a Student Development Educator at Longwood College since completing my PhD in 1986, a naturalistic inquiry ala Lincoln & Guba on sensemaking in a school of education.

I am in the process of trying to secure a publisher. I would like to believe I would have something for one by December, 1990. (But, as Egon says, "Things always take longer than they do!") YOUR TASK, SHOULD YOU CHOOSE TO ACCEPT IT, is to spend an hour of your time and 'talk' to me about the form of your thesis and the questions and answers that led to its structure. Please answer the questions I posed earlier and others you think might be important. Supporting material, e.g., a copy of a table, an example of data display, a table of contents, a page of text, would be gratefully accepted.

THE ONLY REQUIREMENT I have is that you provide at the top of your effort the complete REFERENCE of your work. Any examples ought to have page numbers, etc. I assume much of my task will be to effectively display some of your thoughts. In return, I will promise you to be accurate with my use of your material; to check any assumptions or questions I have about interpreting your material with you. Therefore, please provide a phone number where I might reach you early evening/Saturday mornings (I will not abuse it). I will also send you drafts where your material is explicitly used. I will include you, whether directly cited or not, in the BIBLIOGRAPHY at the back. I might also include a current address **WITH YOUR PERMISSION**, in case any reader wants to be in touch with you directly about your study. IN CONCLUSION, let me give you my office and home phone numbers....

Sincerely,

Letter of Permission

January 14, 1991

I, _____, give permission to Judith M. Meloy, to use the materials I have sent her in the compilation of her volume on the structure and format of qualitative dissertations. I have checked the following (any/all):

1.   I expect to be cited if I am quoted directly, if it is a quote of a sentence or more_____
2.   I prefer to remain anonymous, even if quoted directly_____
3.   I expect to preview any portions of text where I am quoted directly and given credit_____
4.   I give Judith permission to use phrases of two or three words from my effort without expecting to be cited directly_____

(I am thinking of a way to give credit here, like a footnote without using your names, or, simply using first names in parentheses? You don't think THIS format will have trouble getting published!!! e.g.: One of the concerns doctoral students have, regardless of their choice of research paradigm, is 'getting through the maze of institutional barbed wire' [Pat]. How does that suit you-all?)

5.   I give Judith permission to include me generically, without attribution, under phrases such as 'some of the participants', 'several of the writers', etc._____
6.   Other:

                                    SIGNATURE:
                                    Date:

I, Judith M. Meloy, promise to honor your words and meanings in the project on the structure and format of qualitative dissertations. I promise to cite you directly and include you in the Appendix, with the full information you provide, unless you indicate that you wish to remain anonymous. I promise to keep a detailed audit trail, so that all our thoughts, when woven together, are pieces of a greater whole. I promise to do my best in writing a concise, useful volume, which enables other students to undertake qualitative dissertation research with a broader perspective and informs graduate committees of the concerns and issues surrounding such an effort.

January 14, 1991

APPENDIX B:
About the Research Correspondents

Lew Allen, EdD (1992). *Shared Governance: A Case Study of a Primary School.* University of Georgia. Current Position: Director of Outreach of Programs for School Improvement, University of Georgia, G-9 Alderhold Hall, Athens, GA 30602.

Ann, a doctoral student. ["Ann" is a pseudonym. I am grateful to be able to use her letters. Per her request, I have removed any significant references to place or topic.] Address: c/o J. Meloy, P. O. Box 187, Poultney, VT 06764.

Anonymous

Carol, EdD (1989). [Although I had early permission from "Carol" to use her material, we have lost contact. Therefore, I have chosen to use some of the material with "Carol" as the attached pseudonym.]

Robert M. Foster, EdD (1988). *One Good School: A Study of an Effective Elementary School using Ethnographic Research Methods.* Lehigh University. Research Interest: site-based school management. Current Position: Principal, McKinley & Lehigh Parkway Elementary Schools, Bethlehem, PA. Current Address: 326 Carver Drive, Bethlehem, PA 18017.

Pat M. Garlikov, PhD (1990). *Block Play in Kindergarten: A Naturalistic Study.* University of Alabama-Birmingham. Current Position: Assistant Professor, Education, Troy State, Dothen, AL. Current Address: 3300 Burning Tree Drive, Birmingham, AL 35226. "I have spent 20 years in primary classrooms trying to build positive learning environments for kids. I am a mother of two daughters, Lydia and Megan; I am also supported by a curious, thoughtful husband, Rick."

Patricia Kovel-Jarboe, PhD (1986). *An Analysis of Organizational Culture During Change.* University of Minnesota. Research Interest: organizational change and organizational restructuring. Current Position: Coordinator for Quality Improvement, Office of Academic Affairs, University of Minnesota, St. Paul, MN

55108. "I still try to conduct and write my research in ways that are meaningful to the 'subjects' as well as the academic community."

Timothy McCollum, graduate student, University of Georgia. "Looking back at these quotes and comments, I am struck by how much they came back to haunt me in the final months of the project. Perhaps you should have a chapter or something about those uncontrollable/inexplicable events that seem to crop up about the time you begin to see the end of the project."

Marie Wilson Nelson, EdD (1982). *Writers who Teach: A Naturalistic Investigation.* University of Georgia. Research Interests: qualitative (postparadigm shift) assessment/grading/evaluation; women's ways of interacting. Current Position: Assistant Professor, Education, National-Louis University, Tampa Center, FL. Current Address: 1508 Georgia Ave., Tampa, FL 33629-6106.

Kristin Park, PhD (1992). *To Aid the Stranger in Our Midst: Sacrifice, Religiosity, and Gratitude in Three Sanctuary Churches.* University of North Carolina, Chapel Hill. Research Interests: sociology of religion; qualitative methods and societal development and change in Latin America. Current Position and Address: Assistant Professor of Sociology, Westminster College, New Wilmington, PA 16172.

Jane F. Patton, EdD (1991). *A Case Study of a Community College's Program of Cultural Pluralism.* University of Southern California. Research Interest: multicultural higher education. Current Position and Address: Chair, Speech Communication Dept., Mission College, 3000 Mission Blvd., Santa Clara, CA 95054. "As a recent EdD recipient, I'm still trying to figure out what I want to be when I grow up. Currently at a community college, I do want to move to a school of education. P.S. My dissertation did receive a School of Education award for 'outstanding dissertation'!"

Paula Gastenveld Payne, EdD (1990). *Power Communication Skills in Three Female College Presidents: A Descriptive Study.* Vanderbilt University. Research Interests: women's issues, leadership skills, and continuing education. Current Position: Assistant Director Regional Programs, Northeastern Ohio Universities College of Medicine, Rootstown, OH. Current Address: 22 Thirty Acres, Apt. A., Hudson, OH 44236.

Maria Piantanida, PhD (1982). *The Practice of Hospital Education: A Grounded Theory Study.* University of Pittsburgh. Current Position and Address: President, Quality Learning Systems, 2506 Hollywood Drive, Pittsburgh, PA 15235. "I am the principal consultant in my own consulting firm. I specialize in the design of curricula for professionals in health and human services. I have consulted on projects for the Pennsylvania Department of Aging, the University of Pittsburgh, and The Video Difference, Inc., to name a few. I am currently involved in a writing project on the use of portfolios in professional education. Because of my deep belief in the importance of doctoral research, I participate in a 'second generation' Dissertation Study Group where all members are conducting interpretive studies."

Gretchen S. Rauschenberg, PhD (1986). *Reducing Equivocality and Assembling Summaries: A Weickian Analysis of the Information Organizing Processes of a North Central Association On-Site Evaluation Team.* Ohio University. Research Interests: organizational communication; conflict mediation; adult education, training, and development. Current Position and Address: Assistant Professor, Ohio State University, University Drive, Newark, OH 43055.

Kathy Rojek, EdD (1991). *Teachers as Decision Makers in a District-Wide Project.* University of Georgia. Research Interests: change, restructuring, and the teaching profession. Current Position and Address: Elementary Curriculum Coordinator, Barrow County Schools, 109 Church Street, Winder, GA 30680.

Helen Rolfe, PhD (1990). *Case Studies of the Implementation of an Instructional Change in Two Elementary Schools.* University of Virginia. Current Position and Address: Director of Instruction and Professional Development, Virginia Education Association, 116 S. 3rd Street, Richmond, VA 23219. "I am working with 11 pairs of teachers on developing, implementing and disseminating information on alternative forms of assessment in mathematics and science. The project is jointly sponsored by VEA-NEA-Appalachia Ed. Lab—VA Dept. of Education. I am also offering training in the process of change to groups of educators working to restructure their school organizations and programs "

Kathryn A. Scherck, DNSc, RN (1989). *Coping with Acute Myocardial Infarction.* Rush University. Research Interests: coping with AMI, coping with illness; qualitative methods. Current Position: Assistant Professor, Illinois Wesleyan University, Bloomington, IL. Current Address: 9 Golf Pointe Court, Bloomington, IL 61704. "I teach adult critical care and med/surg nursing to undergraduate students. I have a husband, son and cat who are all cited in my dissertation for their support."

Stuart J. Sigman, PhD (1982). *Some Communicational Aspects of Patient Placement and Careers in Two Nursing Homes.* University of Pennsylvania. Current Position and Address: Associate Professor and Chair, Department of Communication, State University of New York at Albany, Albany, NY 12222. "I edit one journal, 'Research on Language and Social Interaction,' and am the author of one book, *A Perspective on Social Communication.* I am interested in developing communication theory sensitive to social and cultural issues."

Jean M. Stevenson, PhD (1989). *The Writing Processes of Theodore Taylor and Jane Yolen.* University of North Dakota. Address: c/o J. Meloy, P. O. Box 187, Poultney, VT 05764. "My research and writing are concentrated in several areas and reflect my interests in whole language; children's literature; the writing processes of writers who write for children and young adults; the evolving nature of the reading and writing processes of children; children's ways of knowing using observations and methods learned through work with Drs. Pat Carini and Sara Hanhan and the Prospect Archive of Children's Work; holistic evaluation and portfolio assessment as viable alternatives to standardized testing; and teachers as researchers in their classrooms."

"I am also the wife of a mineralogist and mother of three children in grades 12, 9, and 7. I am a storyteller and in my free time visit classrooms to tell stories (with the help of my dragons, Horace and Palenknight) and share the writing processes of professional writers with young and not so young writers."

Nancy Zeller, PhD (1987). *A Rhetoric for Naturalistic Inquiry*. Indiana University. Research Interests: educational/social science research rhetoric; narrative use in research on teaching. Current Position and Address: Assistant Professor, School of Education, East Carolina University, Greenville, NC 27858-4353.

APPENDIX C:
Tables of Contents

The tables of content offered in this appendix will provoke a number of questions, including:

- Why are NONE of the formats the same?
- What is the official order of presentation according to your graduate school and/or style manual?
- Is it wise to simply copy the format from someone's dissertation references without checking? (HINT: Probably not...I had looked at several dissertations, rather than at the style manual, because I found it difficult to use as a beginner. Be smarter than I was! Practice with your style manual earlier than I did).
- Where's the raw data, if any?
- Check out the notion of chapter summaries and notes. Is this useful or acceptable?
- What goes in an appendix? What belongs in the body of the thesis?

EXAMPLE 1

Dissertation: *A Case Study of A Community College's Program of Cultural Pluralism.* Jane F. Patton, University of Southern California, May 1991.

DRAFT VERSION
submitted in a letter dated 6/24/90

TABLE OF CONTENTS

Tables & Graphs

CHAPTER I   INTRODUCTION
Background
    External influences on institutions (Changing demographics, statewide
        trends, etc.)
    Mission College: Description (programs, populations, demographics)
        Internal influences on institution (inside the district)
Evolution of the CP Program
    Initial request from Board of Trustees
    First committee: Its study & report 1986–87
    Board approval or report & directive to college
    Program Implementation:
        C.P. Program 1987–8
        C.P. Program 1988–9
        C.P. Program 1989–90
        C.P. Program throughout the college 1986–90
            (review/summary??)
Purpose of Study
Research Questions

CHAPTER II   A Review of the Literature
How multicultural education has been used in institutions of higher education
(weak wording)
    Definition of terms
    Universities (nationally; in California)
    Community Colleges (nationally; in California)

CHAPTER III   Research Methods, Data Collection & Analyses
Data Collected:
    Survey Questionnaire
    Interviews
    Document analyses (list some?)
Data Analyses:
    (Case study methods; qualitative methods; computer programs used; how
        analyzed)

CHAPTER IV   Findings & Data Analyses
From survey questionnaire

<u>From interviews</u>
   with faculty
   with students
   with trustees
   with administrators
<u>From document analyses</u>

CHAPTER V   Conclusions & Recommendations

REFERENCES

APPENDICES
   <u>Survey Questionnaire to Faculty</u>
   <u>Interview Questions</u>: Faculty, Students, Administrators, Trustees
   <u>Documents</u>: Reports to the Board, CP Committee minutes, Curriculum Com-
      mittee....(??) etc.

EXAMPLE 2

Jane Patton's REVISED, ALMOST FINAL version
submitted in a letter dated 2/3/91

IV. FINDINGS
   Introduction
   Mission College: Past and Present
   The Content of CP Program
      Evolution of the CP Program: 1986–90
   How CP is defined
   Perceived goals of the CP program
   Perceptions about the need for a program of CP
   Perceptions about who the CP program is for
   Reactions to Mission's CP Program
      Mission's approach versus an ethnic studies course requirement
   Other Issues related to the CP program
   Who should be responsible for the CP program
   Perceived relevance of CP to various groups
   Outcomes of the CP Program
      Changes reported by faculty members
      Changes noted in course outlines
      Students' observations about CP in classes
      Perceptions about program's accomplishments
      Perceived weaknesses of the program
      Institutionalization of the program
      Perceptions about the future and transferability of the program
      Views of Assimilation
   Conclusions

V. A NEW MODEL OF MULTICULTURAL EDUCATION IN HIGHER
   EDUCATION

REFERENCES

APPENDICES
   A. Survey Questionnaire to Faculty with the response rate for each question
   B. Interview Questions for Faculty
   C. Interview Questions for Students
   D. Interview Questions for Administrators
   E. Interview Questions for Trustees
   F. Report to the Board (more will be added)

EXAMPLE 3

Dissertation: *A Rhetoric for Naturalistic Inquiry*. Nancy Zeller, Indiana
University, 1987.
FINAL version submitted in a letter dated 6/27/90

Table of Contents

EXAMPLE 4

Dissertation: *Organizational Sensemaking: A Study from the Inside Out*. Judith
M. Meloy, Indiana University, July 1986.

FINAL version
July 1986

Title Page
Acceptance Page
Copyright Page
Acknowledgments and Dedication
Foreword

TABLE OF CONTENTS

Chapter
  I. DESCRIPTION OF THE PROBLEM
     The Problem: Context
     The Problem: Focus
     Purposes and Objectives
     Questions to Guide Sensemaking
     Procedures
        Data Source
        Data Base and Data Focus
        Conceptual Framework
        Data Collection
        Data Analyses
        Trustworthiness
     Summary

 II. THE INTERVIEW CASE REPORTS
     Interview Case Report, Respondent B.
     Interview Case Report, Respondent C.
     Interview Case Report, Respondent D.
     Interview Case Report, Respondent E.
     Interview Case Report, Respondent F.
     Interview Case Report, Respondent G.
     Interview Case Report, Respondent H.
     Interview Case Report, Respondent J.

III. THE FINAL ANALYSIS
     Overall Impressions—A General Sense
        Lens One: Language
        Lens Two: Structure
        Lens Three: Assertion and Assumption
        Summary
     Specific Impressions—Particular Approaches to Sensemaking

EXAMPLE 5

Dissertation: *Some Communicational Aspects of Patient Placement and Careers in Two Nursing Homes*. Stuart Jay Sigman, University of Pennsylvania, 1982.

FINAL version
submitted in a letter dated 5/2/90

TABLE OF CONTENTS

Conclusions and Discussion
NOTES

APPENDIX: RESEARCH DOCUMENTS

INDEX

BIBLIOGRAPHY

LIST OF TABLES

LIST OF FIGURES

BIBLIOGRAPHY

Barone, T. (1992a). Beyond theory and method: A case of critical storytelling. *Theory into Practice, 31*(2), 142–146.

Barone, T. (1992b). On the demise of subjectivity in educational inquiry. *Curriculum Inquiry, 22*(1), 25–38.

Barone, T. (in press). Breaking the mold: The new American student as strong poet. *Theory into Practice.*

Bogdan, R., & Biklen, S. (1982). *Qualitative research for education: An introduction to theory and methods.* Needham Heights, MA: Allyn & Bacon.

Calkins, L. (1983). *Lessons from a child: On the teaching and learning of writing.* Portsmouth, NH: Heinemann Press.

Carter, K. (1993). The place of story in the study of teaching and teacher education. *Educational Researcher, 22*(1), 5–12.

Eisner, E. W. (1991). *The enlightened eye.* New York: Macmillan.

Eisner, E. W. (1993, April 14). *Forms of understanding and the future of educational research.* Presidential address of the annual conference of the American Educational Research Association, Atlanta.

Eisner, E. W., & Peshkin, A. (Eds). (1990). *Qualitative inquiry in education: The continuing debate.* New York: Teachers College Press.

Ely, M. (1991). *Doing qualitative research: Circles within circles.* London: Falmer Press.

Glaser, B. G., & Strauss, L. (1967). *The discovery of grounded theory.* New York: Aldine de Gruyter.

Glesne, C., & Peshkin, A. (1992). *Becoming qualitative researchers: An introduction.* New York: Longman.

Goetz, J. P., & LeCompte, M. D. (1984). *Ethnography and qualitative design in educational research.* Orlando: Academic Press.

Guba, E. G. (Ed.). (1990). *The paradigm dialog.* Newbury Park, CA: Sage.

Guba, E. G., & Lincoln, Y. S. (1981). *Effective evaluation.* San Francisco: Jossey-Bass.

Halpern, E., & Schwandt, T. (1988). *Linking auditing and metaevaluation: Enhancing quality in applied research.* Newbury Park, CA: Sage.

Heller, J. (1974). *Something happened.* New York: Knopf.

Ives, E. D. (1980). *The tape-recorded interview: A manual for field workers in folklore and oral history.* Knoxville: University of Tennessee Press.

Larson, C. (1992, April). *Self-representation in biographical and autobiographical narrative: Disclosing the assumptions of the inquirer.* Paper presented at the annual conference of the American Educational Research Association, San Francisco.

Lincoln, Y. S., & Guba, E. G. (1985). *Naturalistic inquiry.* Beverly Hills: Sage.

Marshall, C., & Rossman, G. (1989). *Designing qualitative research.* Beverly Hills: Sage.

Meloy, J. M. (1986). *Organizational sensemaking: A study from the inside out.* Unpublished doctoral dissertation, Indiana University, Bloomington.

Meloy, J. M. (1992, April). *Writing the qualitative dissertation: Voices of experience.* Paper presented at the annual conference of the American Educational Research Association, San Francisco.

Meloy, J. M. (1993). Problems of writing and representation in qualitative inquiry. *International Journal of Qualitative Studies in Education, 6*(4), 315–330.

Merriam, S. B. (1991). *Case study research in education: A qualitative approach.* San Francisco: Jossey-Bass.

Merryfield, M. (1992). *Constructing scenes and dialogues to display findings in case study reporting.* Paper presented at the annual conference of Qualitative Research in Education, Athens, GA.

Mishler, E. G. (1986). *Research interviewing: Context and narrative.* Cambridge, MA: Harvard University Press.

Morgan, G. (1983). *Beyond method.* Beverly Hills: Sage.

Nelson, M. (1991). *At the point of need: Teaching basic and ESL writers.* Portsmouth, NH: Boynton/Cook.

Pike, K. (1967). *Language in relation to a unified theory of the structure of human behavior.* The Hague, Netherlands: Mouton.

Richardson, L. (1990). *Writing strategies.* Newbury Park, CA: Sage.

Rosenblatt, L. (1978). *The reader, the text, the poem.* Carbondale: Southern Illinois University Press.

Schatzman, L., & Strauss, A. (1973). *Field research: Strategies for a natural sociology.* Englewood Cliffs, NJ: Prentice-Hall.

Smith, J. K. (1988, March). The evaluator/researcher as person vs. the person as evaluator/researcher. *Educational Researcher, 17*(2), 18–23.

Smith, J. K. (1992, April). *The stories educational researchers tell about themselves.* Paper presented at the annual conference of the American Educational Research Association, San Francisco.

Taylor, V., & Bonham, A. (1992, January). *Gaining access to bureaucratic organizations.* Workshop presented at the annual conference on Qualitative Research in Education, University of Georgia, Athens.

Weick, K. (1979). *The social psychology of organizing* (2nd ed.). New York: Random House.

Wolcott, H. (1990). *Writing up qualitative research.* Newbury Park, CA: Sage.

Yin, R. K. (1984). *Case study research.* Newbury Park, CA: Sage.

Zeller, N. (1987). *A rhetoric for naturalistic inquiry.* Unpublished doctoral dissertation, Indiana University, Bloomington.

Zeller, N. (1990, July 6). *A rhetoric for naturalistic inquiry: Writing the case report.* Paper presented at the University of Iowa Conference on Narrative in the Human Sciences, Iowa City.

INDEX